Paul Leicester Ford

Check list of Bibliographies, Catalogues, Reference Lists, and Lists of Authorities of American Books and Subjects

Paul Leicester Ford

Check list of Bibliographies, Catalogues, Reference Lists, and Lists of Authorities of American Books and Subjects

ISBN/EAN: 9783337279325

Printed in Europe, USA, Canada, Australia, Japan

Cover: Foto ©Andreas Hilbeck / pixelio.de

More available books at **www.hansebooks.com**

Check List of Bibliographies, Catalogues, Reference-Lists, and Lists of Authorities of American Books and Subjects

COMPILED BY

PAUL LEICESTER FORD

———

BROOKLYN, N. Y.
1889

TO
JUSTIN WINSOR,
WHOSE NAME OCCURS OFTENEST IN THIS LIST,

I DEDICATE IT,

AS SOME RECOGNITION OF HIS WORK IN

AMERICAN BIBLIOGRAPHY.

NOTE.

IN the following list I have included only such library, auction, and booksellers' catalogues as appear to me to have a real value for reference, either from the character of the collection, the method of arrangement, the careful cataloguing, or annotating.

The letter to the left of the number denotes the character of the work, thus :

A signifies Auction Sale Catalogue.
B   "   Bibliography.
C   "   Booksellers' Catalogue.
L   "   Public Library Catalogue.
P   "   Private Library Catalogue.
R   "   Reference List,
W   "   List of writers.

And the sign to the right shows the method of arrangement, thus :

* signifies arranged Alphabetically, by authors.
†   "   "   Alphabetically, by subjects.
‡   "   "   Chronologically.
‖   "   "   Classically.

Where two or more signs are used, the first shows the method of arrangement, and those that follow indicate indexes on whatever system the sign denotes.

These brief titles are designed as the working basis for a full and critical catalogue of Bibliographies, Catalogues, Reference Lists, and Lists of Authorities of American books and subjects, and I shall be grateful for any additions or corrections. I am under obligation to Mr. W. Eames, Mr. W: C. Lane, Mr. C: A. Nelson, and to all the authors of the class of Bibliography herein, for assistance in the compilation.

CLASSIFICATION OF CONTENTS.

Bibliography.

CARR, H. J. Index to some recent Reference Lists, [in Library Journal, VIII, p. 27]. New York : 1883.   R 1 †

[COGSWELL, J. G.] List of Bibliographies, [in Index to the Astor Library, p. v]. New York : 1851.   R 2 †

CUTTER, C. A. Bibliografy of Bibliography, [in Library Journal, each issue]. New York : 1876–1887.   B 3

FOSTER, W. E. Report on aids and guides to readers, [in Library Journal, VIII, p. 233]. New York : 1883.   R 4 |

GUILD, R. A. Bibliography of Bibliography, [in The Librarians' Manual, p. 1]. New York : 1858.   B 5 *

[HARRISSE, H.] Bibliographies relating to America, [in Bibliotheca Am. Vetustissima, p. x]. New York : 1866.   B 6 ‡ †

HOMES, H. A. Catalogue of Books on Bibliography, etc., in the New York State Library. Albany : 1858.   B 8 * †

— — Bibliography, [in Subject Index, New York State Library, p. 48]. Albany : 1872.   R. 9 |

— — same, [in Supplement, p. 28]. Albany : 1882.   R 70 |

INDEX to special book lists found in the Catalogue of the Boston Public Library and other libraries, and also in periodicals, [in B. P. L. Bulletin, V, p. 444]. Boston : 1883.   R 7 †

JACKSON, J. List Provisoire de Bibliographies Géographies Spéciales. Paris : 1881. B 11 | *

LANE, W. C. Index to recent Reference Lists, 1884–5. Cambridge : 1885.   R 12 †
Same in Harvard Bulletin. 1886.

— — Index to recent Reference Lists. 1885–6. Cambridge : 1887.   R 13 †
Same in Harvard Bulletin. 1886.

[LEYPOLDT, F.] List of the most recent works on Bibliography, [in Publishers and Stationers' Weekly Trade Circular, II (new series), p. 418]. New York : 1872.   B 14 †

LEYPOLDT, F. Bibliographic aids, [in American Catalogue, II, p. v]. New York : 1881. B 15 †

LIST of Auction sales Catalogues, [in Bookmart II, p. 550]. Pittsburg : 1885.   R 16 *

LUDEWIG, H. E. A survey of the bibliographical sources which relate to books on America, [in Naumann's Serapæum, July 31]. Leipzig : 1845.   17

PETZHOLDT, J. Bibliotheca Bibliographica. Leipzig : 1866.   B 18 | *

POOLE, W. F. List of Bibliographies, [in Find-ing List of the Chicago Public Library, p. 345.] Chicago : 1884.   R 19 *

[PORTER, G. W.] Hand-list of Bibliographies [etc.] in the Reading-Room of the British Mu-seum. [London :] 1881.   B 20 | *

POWER, J. Bibliography of Bibliography, [in A Handy book about books, p. 1.] London : 1870.   B 21 *

SABIN, J. Bibliography of Bibliography. New York : 1877.   B 22 *

SPOFFORD, A. R. Bibliography of Bibliography and Literature, [in Public Libraries in the U. S., I, p. 689]. Washington : 1876.   B 23 |

TRÜBNER, N. [& Ludewig, H. E.] Bibliograph-ical works relating to America, [in Trübner's Bibliographical Guide to Ameri n Literature, p. 1]. London : 1859.   B 24 ‡ *

VALLÉE, L. Bibliographie des Bibliographies. Paris : 1883.   B 25 * †

— — Bibliographie des Bibliographies. Supple-ment. Paris : 1887.   B 26 * †

Subject Catalogues and " Finding Lists."

ASTOR Library. Alphabetical Index to. New York : 1851.   27 (1)

BOSTON Athenæum. Catalogue of the Library of. Boston : 1872-82.   27 (2)

BRITISH Museum. Subject Index of Modern Works added to. London : 1886.   28

BROOKLYN Library. Analytical and classed cat-alogue of. Brooklyn : 1878-80.   29

BRUNET, J. C. Manuel du Libraire, Tome VI. [subjects]. Paris : 1865.   30

CINCINNATI. Finding list of books in the Public Library of. Cincinnati : 1884.   31

CHICAGO Public Library. Finding list of. Chi-cago : 1884-87.   32

COLLEGE of New Jersey. Subject Catalogue of. New York : 1884.   33

CONGRESS. Catalogue of the Library of. Wash-ington : 1861.   34

— same Index of Subjects. Washington : 1869.   35

NEW YORK State Library. Subject Index. Al-bany : 1872.   36

— — Supplement. Albany : 1882.   37

PHILADELPHIA. Catalogue of the books of the Library Company of Philadelphia. Philadel-phia : 1835-1846.   38

PEABODY Institute. Catalogue of the Library of. Baltimore : 1883.   39

ROYAL Geographical Society. Classified Cata-logue of. London : 1871.   41

ST. LOUIS Mercantile Library. Classified Cat-alogue of. St. Louis : 1874.   41

WATT, R. Bibliotheca Britannica. [Subject Index, Vols. III and IV.] Edinburg : 1824. 42

America in General.

Many works which purport to treat of "America" use the word in its narrow sense and are placed herein under "Political Divisions, United States."

ALCEDO, A. de. List of books, etc., on America, [in Geo. and Hist. dictionary of America, I, p. xxv]. London : 1812. 43

ALLIBONE, S. A. A Critical Dictionary of English and American Authors. Philadelphia : 1859–71. B 44 *

ALOFSEN, S. Works on America, [in Catalogues de Livres, etc. of, p. i]. Utrecht : 1876. A 45 (1)|

AMERICAN Antiquarian Society. Catalogue of books in. Worcester : 1837. L 45 (2) *

[ASHER, G. M.] Catalogue of Books relating to America. [Amsterdam : 1850.] C 46 |

ASHER, G. M. A Bibliographical Essay on Dutch books relating to New Netherland, the Dutch West India Company, Brazil, Angola, etc. Amsterdam : 1854–67. B 47 | *

ASPINWALL, T. Catalogue of Books relating to America. Paris : 1838. P 48

BARLOW, S. L. M., and Harrisse, H. Bibliotheca Barlowiana. New York : 1864. P 49

[BARCIA, A. G.] Works on North America, [in Esayo Chronologico para la historia de la Florida, by G. De Cardenas z Cano]. Madrid : 1722. 5c

BARRAS Arana, D. Notas para una bibliografia de obras anónimas e seudónimas sobre América. Santiago : 1882. B 51

BARTLETT, J. R. Bibliotheca Americana. A Catalogue of Books in the Library of John Carter Brown. [4 vols.] Providence : 1866–1875. P 52 ‡ *

[BARTLETT, J. R.] Catalogue of the Library of Henry C. Murphy. [Providence :] 1884. A 53 *

BOONE, E. P. Catalogue of Americana. New York : 1870. A 54

BOSSANGE, H. Ma Bibliothèque Américaine. Paris : 186–. 55

BRITISH Museum. List of works relating to America, [in Cat. of Printed books, I, 157]. London : 1882. 56

CALLE, J. Diez de la. Biblioteca Americana. 1646. B 57

CATALOGUE d'un choix de livres relatifs à l'Amérique. Paris : 1857. A 58 *

CATALOGUE of books relating to the history of America, in the library of the legislative assembly of Canada. Montreal : 1845. L 59 |

CATALOGUE of the library of Parliament. Works relating to America. Toronto : 1858. L 60 |

CHARLEVOIX, P. F. X. de. Critical List of authors cited, [in Histoire ... de la Nouvelle France, I]. Paris : 1744. B 61 ‡
Also in Shea's reprint, N. Y.: 1866.

CLARKE, R. Bibliotheca Americana. Cincinnati : 1875. C 62 * †

— — Bibliotheca Americana. Cincinnati : 1876.

CLARKE, R. Bibliotheca Americana. Cincinnati :
1878.   C 64 |
— — Supplement. Cincinnati : 1878.   C 65 *
— — Bibliotheca Americana. Cincinnati : 1883.
                                              C 66 |
— — Bibliotheca Americana. Cincinnati : 1886.
                                              C 67 |
— — Supplement. Cincinnati : 1887.   C 68 |

COOKE, J. J. Catalogue of the Library of. Part
III, Americana.' New York : 1883.   A 69 *

DENHAM, A. Catalogue of the Library of C. I.
Bushnell. New York : 1883.   A 70 *

DRAUDIUS, G. De Scriptoribus Rerum Ameri-
canarum. [in Bibliotheca Classica]. Franco-
furti : 1622.   71

DUFOSSÉ, E. Bulletin du Bouquiniste. Americana. Paris : 1876–1887.   C 72 *

FALCONET, M. Works on America, [in Cat. de la
Bibliothèque de, p. 363]. Paris: 1763. A 72 (1)

FARIBAULT, G. B. Catalogue d'Ouvrage sur
l'Histoire de l'Amérique, et en particulier sur
Canada, Louisiane, Arcadie et autres lieux.
Québec : 1837.   B 73 * ‡

FASSO, P. List of Authors used, [in De Regio
patronatu Indiarum, I, p. xxi]. Matriti: 1775.
                                              R 74

FERRARIO, J. Bibliography of works relating to
America, [in Le costume ancien et moderne,
XVI, p. 65]. Milan : 1827.   B 74 (1) *

GARCIA, G. List of Authors used, [in Origen
de los Indios, p. 11.] Madrid : 1727.   75

GUILD, C. H. Catalogue of the Library of.
Boston : 1887.   A 76 *

[HARRISSE, H.] Bibliotheca Americana Vetustissima. New York : 1866.   B 77 ‡ *

[— —] Additions. Paris : 1872.   B 78 ‡ *

[— —] Introduccion de la imprenta en América,
con una bibliografiá de las obras impresa desde
1540 à 1600. Madrid : 1872.   B 79 ‡

HERRERA, A. de. List of Authors who have
written on the West Indies, [in Historia general de las Indias Occidentales, I, p. 5]. Am-
beres : 1728.   80
     Also in English edition of 1725 and Spanish of 1730.

HOLMES, A. Catalogue of Authorities, [in Annals of America, 2d ed. I, p. ix]. Cambridge :
1829.   B 81 *

IRWIN, T. Catalogue of the Library of. New
York : 1887.   P 82 *

[KENNETT, W., and WATTS, R.] Bibliothecæ
Americanæ Primordia. London : 1713.
                                      B 83 ‡ *

LAET, J. de. List of works on America, [in
Nieuwe Wereldt, p. 12]. Leyden : 1625.
                                      B 84 |

LECLERC, C. Bibliotheca Americana. Paris :
1867.   A 85 *

— — Catalogue of books on America, [in Bibliotheca Historica, p. 80]. Paris : 1869. A 86 *

— — Bibliotheca Americana. [3 parts.] Paris :
1878–1887.   C 87 | * ‡

[LENOX, J.] Livres Curieux. New York : 1854.
88

LEON-PINELO, A. de. Epitome de la Biblioteca Oriental i Occidental, Nautica, i Geografica. Madrid : 1629. B 89

— — [Second edition, enlarged by A. C. Barcia. 3 vols.] Madrid : 1737–8. B 90

MARTENS, C. de. Works on America, [in Guide Diplomatique, I, bis p. 575]. Paris : 1837. B 91 (1)

MASSACHUSETTS HISTORICAL SOCIETY. Catalogue of the Library of. Boston : 1859. L 91 (2)*

MENCKE, J. B. List of Works on America, [in Catalogue des principaux historiens, p. 426.] Leipzig : 1714. 92

MORSE, Jedediah. List of Authorities. [American Gazetteer.] Boston : 1797. R 93

MULLER, F. Catalogue of Books on America. [6 parts.] Amsterdam : 1872–75. C 94 |

— — Catalogue of Books relating to America. Amsterdam : 1877. C 95 *

— — Rough list of Spanish books chiefly relating to America. [Amsterdam : n. d.] C 96

[MURPHY, H. C.] A Catalogue of an American Library, chronologically arranged. Brooklyn: 1850. R 97 ‡

NASH, E. W. Catalogue of the Library of E. B. O'Callaghan. New York : 1882. C 98 *

NEW YORK Historical Society. Catalogue of books in the Library of. [By G. H. Moore.] New York : 1859. L 99 (1) *

NORTON, C. B. Catalogue of books relating to America. New York : 1862. C 99 (2) |

OGILBY, J. A Catalogue of Authors who have written on America, [in America : being a description of the new world, p. 5]. London : 1671. 100

PRINCE, T. Catalogue of the American portion of the Library of. Boston : 1868. L 101 *

QUARITCH, B. No. 259. Bibliotheca Occidentalis. London : 1870. C 102 |

— — No. 286. Bibliotheca Occidentalis. London : 1873. C 103 *

— — No. 294. Catalogues of Voyages and Travels and Works relating to America. London : 1875. C 104 *

— — No. 363, II. Catalogue of the Hist., Geog. and Philology of American. London : 1885 C 105 *

— — No. 46. Rough list of books relating to America. London : 1880. C 106 *

— — Catalogue of books on the History, Geography, and Philology of America. London : 1886. C 107

See also under America — Geography.

RAFINESQUE, C. S. Catalogue of Authorities, [in Ancient History, or, annals of Kentucky, p. 38]. Frankfort, Ky.: 1824. R 108

— — "Materials" for American History, [in The American Nations, p. 35]. Philadelphia : 1836. R 109

[REID, —— ?] Bibliotheca Americana. London:
1789.   B 110 ‡

[RICH, O.] A Catalogue of Books relating to
America. London : 1832.   C 111 ‡

RICH, O. Bibliotheca Americana Nova. London : 1835–46.   B 112 ‡

ROBERTSON, W. Catalogue of Spanish Books
and Manuscripts relating to America, [in History of America, p. 523]. London : 1777.
                                             B 113 *

SABIN, J., [and Eames, W.] A Dictionary of
Books relating to America. New York : 1868.
                                             B 114 *

SABIN, J. Catalogue of John A. Rice's Library.
New York : 1870.   A 115 * †

— — Catalogue of William Menzies. New York:
1875.   A 116 *

— — Catalogue of the Library of Francis Hoff-
man. New York : 1877.   A 117 *

— — Catalogue of the Library of T. A. Emmett.
New York : 1868.   A 118 *

SMITH, J. R. Bibliotheca Americana. London:
1849.   C 119 ‡

— — Bibliotheca Americana. London : 1853.
                                             C 120

— — Bibliotheca Americana. London : 1865.
                                             C 121 * ‡ †

SMITH, A. R. Bibliotheca Americana. London:
1871.   C 122 * †

— — Bibliotheca Americana. London : 1874.
                                             C 123 * †

STEVENS, Henry. Bibliotheca Americana. London: 1861.   A 124 *

— — Historical Nuggets. Bibliotheca Americana. London: 1862.   C 125 *

— — The Humboldt Library. London : 1863.
                                             A 126 *

— — Schedules of 2000 American Historical
Nuggets. London: 1870.   R 127 ‡

— — Catalogue of Books relating to America, in-
cluding the collection of M. Tross. London:
1870.   A 128 *

STEVENS, Henry. Bibliotheca Historica. A catalogue of 5000 volumes relating to America.
Boston : 1870.   A 129 *

— — Bibliotheca Geographica and Historica.
London : 1872.   A 130 *

— — Catalogue [Parts I and II] of Books and
mss. relating to America. London : 1881.
                                             A 131 *

STRUVE, B. G. List of works on America, [in
Bibliotheca Historiæ.] Jena : 1740.   132

— — [same, enlarged by J. G. Mensel.] Lipsiæ :
1782.   133

TERNAUX, H. Bibliothèque Américaine. Paris :
1837.   B 134 ‡

TRÖMEL, P. Bibliothèque Américaine. Leipzig :
1861.   C 135 ‡

[TROSS, E.] Bibliothèque Américaine. Paris :
1873.   C 136 *

TRÜBNER, N. Bibliographical Guide to American Literature. London : 1859.　　B 137 | *
— — Catalogue of books relating to America. London : 1873.　　　　　　C 138 *
[TRUMBULL, J. H.] Catalogue of the American Library of George Brinley. [Parts I–IV.] Hartford : 1878–1887.　　　　　　A 139 |
VICUÑA Mackenna, B. Bibliografía Americana. Valparaiso : 1879.　　　　　　P 140
[WARDEN, D. B.] Bibliotheca Americo Septentrionalis : [Paris :] 1820.　　　P 141 *
— — Bibliotheca Americana. Paris : 1831.
　　　　　　　　　　　　　　　　　P 142 |
　　Also " Paris : 1840."
WINSOR, J., and others. Bibliographic sources of information, [in Narrative and Critical History of America]. Boston : 1882.　　R 143
WOODWARD, W. E. Bibliotheca Americana. Boston : 1869.　　　　　　A 144 *
WRIGHT, J. O. Rough list as a basis of a Catalogue of the library of S. L. M. Barlow. New York : 1885.　　　　　　P 145

ARCHÆOLOGY.

HAVEN, S. F. Archæology of the U. S., or sketches, Historical and Bibliographical. New York: 1856.　　　　　　B 146
　　Also in Smithsonian Contrib. to Knowledge, VIII.

GEOGRAPHY.
(Voyages and Explorations.)

No. 188 contains a Catalogue of Bibliography and Catalogues. *See also* No. 11.

Classed under
　　General Works.
　　Maps.
　　Collected Voyages.
　　For Special Nations, *see* Ethnology.
　　For Special Regions, *see* Political Divisions.
　　For Individual Explorations, *see* Individual.

General Works.

AA, Van der. Catalogue of books on Geography, [in Bibliotheca Selectissima, II, pp. 375]. Amsterdam: 1729.　　　　　　A 147
ASHER, A. List of authorities, [in Henry Hudson, the Navigator]. London: 1861.　B 148
ASHER, G. M. *See* No. 46.
BARLOW, S. L. M. *See* Nos. 49 and 145.
BARTLETT, J. R. *See* Nos. 52 and 53.
BECKMAN, J. Literatur de älterem Reisebeschreibungen. Gottingen: 1807–9.　　B 149
BOEHMER, G. R. List of Voyages, etc., in America, [in Bib. Scriptorum Historiæ Naturalis, I, I]. Lipsiæ: 1785.　　　　　　150
BOUCHER DE LA RICHARDERIE, G. Bibliothèque Universelle des Voyages. Paris: 1808.
　　　　　　　　　　　　　　　　　B 151 | *
BURE, G. F. de. Collections of Voyages and Relations, [in Bibliographie instructive, p. 66]. Paris: 1768.　　　　　　B 152
BUTLER, [J.] List of works on Geography, [in Catalogue of the Library of, p. 303]. London: 1753.　　　　　　A 153

CARERI, G. F. G. Catalogo de' viaggiatori, [in Giro del Mondo, I]. Venezia: 1729.   R 154

CASTELLANI, C. Catalogo Ragionto delle Opere Geografiche a Stampa. Roma: 1877.   B 155

CHANNING, E. Sources of information concerning the Companions of Columbus, [in No. 143, II, 204].   R 156

DISCOVERIES in America. Early History and later Collections, [in Bost. Pub. Library Bull., III, p. 207]. Boston: 1877.   R 157

DIBDIN, T. F. List of Voyages and Travels, [in The Library Companion, p. 376]. London: 1824.   B 158

DU FRESNOY, L. Méthode pour étudier le Geographie. Avec un Catalogue des Cartes Geographiques, de Relations, Voyages et Descriptions. Paris: 1736.   B 159

ENGLEMANN, W. Works on American Geography, [in Bibliotheca Geographica, p. 180]. Leipzig: 1858.   B 160

EARLY Exploration in America, [in Bost. Pub. Lib. Bull., III, pp. 103, 136, 205, and 241]. Boston: 1877.   R 161

EARLY English Exploration in America, [in Monthly Ref. List, IV, p. 27]. N. Y.: 1884.   R 162

FLEURIEU, C. de C. P. Works on Geography, [in Catalogue des livres, p. 68]. Paris: 1810.   A 163

GRIFFIN, A. P. C. Discovery of the Mississippi. Bibliographical Account. Boston: 1883.   R 164

.   Also in Mag. of Am. Hist., IX, pp. 190, 273.

HAKLUYT Society. List of the publications. [London:] 1887.   C 165 ‡

HARRISSE, H. *See* Nos. 77 and 78.

MORISOTO, C. B. List of Authorities, [in Orbis Maritimi, p. 23]. Divione, 1643.   R 166

JONES, J. W. List of Voyages to Virginia, [in Strachey's History of Travaile in Virginia, p. iii]. London: 1849.   B 167

— — List of writers on Geography, [in Hakluyt's Divers voyages touching the discovery of America, p. xlii]. London: 1850.   B 168

LEON PINELO, A. de. *See* Nos. 89 and 90.

LOCKE, J. Catalogue of Voyages and Travels, [in A Collection of Voyages and Travels, I, p. 1]. London: 1744.   B 169 *

   Also in Vol. X of "Works of John Locke. London: 1823," and in "The Progress of Maritime Discovery, by J. S. Clarke, London, 1803," p. 171.

MURR, C. T. de. List of Geographical Works, [in Hist. dip. de Martin Behain]. Nuremburg : 1788.   R 170

MURRAY, Hugh. Bibliography of Voyages and Travels in America, [in Hist. Account of Discov. and Travel in Am.]. London : 1829,   B 171

MULLER, F. Geographical Works on America, [in Catalogues de livres, etc., de N. W. Posthumus, p. 53]. Amsterdam: 1887.   C 172 |

— — See No. 94.

NAVARETTE, M. F. Biblioteca Maritima Española. Madrid: 1851.   B 173

NEILL, E. Sources of information relative to the discovery of the great Lakes, [in No. 143, IV, p. 196]. R 174

PINKERTON, J. Catalogue of books of Voyages and Travels, [in A General Collection of Voyages and Travels, XVII, p. 1]. London: 1814 B 175

PINKERTON, J. Catalogue of Maps and of Books of Voyages and Travels, [in Modern Geography, II, 792]. London: 1811. B 176 |

PURCHAS, S. List of Authorities, [in Purchas his Pilgrimage, p. 23]. London: 1613. W 177 *

— — [Same, enlarged, in 4th edition, V, p. 31]. London: 1626. W 178 *

SAN FILIPO, P. A. de. Bibliografia del Viaggiatori Italiana. Roma: 1874. 179

QUARITCH, B. No. 229. Catalogue of Works on Geography, Travels, Early Discoveries, etc. London: 1866. C 180 |

— — No. 238. Catalogue of Geography, Travels, etc. London: 1867. C 181 *

— — No. 249. Catalogue of Works on Geography, Travel, etc. London: 1869. C 182

— — No. 266. Catalogue of Voyages and Travels. London: 1870. C 183 *

— — No. 294. A New Catalogue of works of Voyages and Travels. London: 1875. C 184 *

— — No. 321. Bibliotheca Geographica-Linguistica. London: 1876. C 185 |

— — See Nos. 102-107.

SAVONAROLA, R. List of works on Geography, [in Universus terrarum Orbis, by A. L. a Varea (pseud.)]. Patavii: 1713. 186

SILVER, S. W. Catalogue of the York Gate Geographical and Colonial Library. London: 1882. P 187 |

— — [same, new edition, greatly enlarged.] London: 1886. P 188 |

STEVENS, H. See No. 130.

STEVENSON, W. Catalogue of Voyages and Travels, [in Kerr's General History and Collection of Voyages, XVIII, p. 529]. London: 1824. B 189 |

TIELE, P. T. Memoire Bibliographique sur les Journeaux des Navigateurs Neerlandais. Amsterdam: 1867. B 190

— — Bibliographie van Nederlandsche Reisebeschrevingen, [in Bibliographische Adversaria, I]. 'S. Gravenhage: 1873. B 191

TRÜBNER, N. See No. 137.

WALCKENAËR, C. A. Catalogue des livres et cartes Géographique de la bibliothèque de. Paris: 1853. A 192

WARDEN, D. B. See No. 139.

WILLIS, W. A bibliographical Essay on the early collections of voyages to America, [in Hist. and Gen. Register XV, p. 205]. Boston: 1861. B 193

Maps.

(See Geology for Geological Maps.)

ASHER, G. M. A List of Maps and Charts of New Netherland. Amsterdam: 1855 B 195

BALDWIN, C. C. Early Maps of Ohio and the West. Cleveland : 1875. B 196

COSTA, B. F. De. Descriptions of 5 charts of America anterior to 1528, [in Sailing directions of Henry Hudson]. Albany : 1869. R 197

CATALOGUE of maps of the U. S. Washington: 1862. L 198

CATALOGUE of the Maps and Surveys in the office of the Secretary of State, of the State Engineer, and of the New York State Library. Albany : 1859. L 199
Earlier edition, Albany : 1851.

CATALOGUE of the N. Y. State Library. Maps, etc. Albany : 1857. L 200

CATALOGUE of Charts in Hydrographic Office of the Bureau of Navigation, U. S. 3 vols. Washington : 1873–76. L 201

CATALOGUE of Map Room of the Royal Geographical Society. London : 1882. L 202

DALL, W. H., and Baker, M. Partial list of Charts, Maps, and Publications relating to Alaska, [in U. S. Coast and Geodetic Survey, p. 163]. Washington : 1879. B 203

DUFOSSÉ, E. See No. 72.

FARIBAULT, G. B. See No. 73.

HALE, E. E. Catalogue of maps and plans of military positions held in the French and Revolutionary Wars, etc. Boston : 186–. C 204

HARRISSE, H. See Political Divisions—Canada.

HAYWARD, John. Maps on New England, [in The New England Gazetteer, 4]. Concord : 1839. B 205

KOHL, J. G. A descriptive catalogue of those maps, charts, and surveys relating to America which are mentioned in Vol. 3 of Hackluyt's great work. Washington : 1857. B 206

LABANOFF DE ROSTOFF, A. Catalogue des Cartes Géographique, etc. Paris : 1823. P 207

LANGE, H. Contributions à la Cartographie de la Province Brezilienne de Santa Catharina, [in Bulletin de la Société de Géographie, 6th ser., vol. 18, p. 430]. Paris: 1879. B 208

MAPS of America, 1540–1600. [Bull. Boston Pub. Lib., III, 205]. Boston : 1877. R 209

MARCEL, G. Cartographie de la Nouvelle France. Supplement à l'ouvrage de M. Harrisse. Paris : 1885. B 210

MULLER, F. Catalogue of Books, etc., on America. Part III, d. Atlases, Maps, Charts, and Globes. Amsterdam : 1875. C 211

MULLER, F. Cartes Generales—l'Amerique, [in Catalogues de Cartes, etc., p. 76]. Amsterdam : 188–. C 212

NORTON, C. B. See No. 99 (2).

OROZCO Y BERRA, M. Materiales para una Cartografia Mexicana, [in Boletin de la Soc. de Geografia]. Mexico: 1871. B 213

QUARITCH, B. See No. 102.

PALFREY, J. G. Maps delineating the New England coast of an earlier date than 1614, [History of N. E., I, 95]. Boston: 1859. R 214

PARKMAN, F. Early unpublished Maps of the Mississippi and the great Lakes, [in France and England in America, III, p. 449]. Boston: 1880. R 215

PATTERSON, C. P.   United States coast and geodetic Survey. Catalogue of charts. Washington: 1886.   L 216
Many prior editions.

PEIRCE, B.   A Catalogue of Maps and Charts in
Harvard University. Cambridge: 1831. L 217

SALKELD, J. Maps and Charts of America, [in
Bib. Americana, Pt. I, p. 39, and Pt. II, p. 42].
London: 1877–1881.   C 218

STEVENS, H. Catalogue of the American Maps
in the British Museum. London: 1856. L 219

THOMASSY, R. Cartographie de l'ancienne Louisiane, [in Geologie pratique de la Louisiane, p.
205]. Paris: 1860.   B 220

TRÜBNER, N. *See* No. 137.

URICOECHEA, E. Mapoteca Colombiana. Lón-
dres: 1860.   B 221

WARDEN, D. B. *See* No. 142.

WARREN, G. K. Maps of the Mississippi, [in
Report on bridging of the Mississippi, p. 1123].
Washington: 1878.   B 222

WINSOR, J. Cartography of Louisiana and the
Mississippi, [in No. 143, V, p. 79].   R 223

— — Early Maps of New-England, [in No. 143,
III, p. 380].   R 224

— — General Atlases and Charts of America of
the 16th and 17th Centuries, [in No. 143, IV,
p. 369].   R 225

— — Maps of Arcadia, [in No. 143, V, p. 472.]
                                              225 (2)

— — Maps of the Eastern Coast of N. A.,
[in No. 143, III, p. 33].   R 226

— — Maps of the North East Coast, [in No. 143,
IV, p. 81].   R 227

— — Maps of the Pacific Coast, [in No. 143, II,
p. 431].   R 228

— — Maps of the 17th Century of Canada, [in
No. 143, IV, p. 377].   R 229

— — Maps of Virginia, [in No. 143, III, p. 167].
                                              R 230

— — The Kohl Collection of Maps relating to
America. Cambridge: 1886.   B 231
Also in Harvard Bulletin, Vols. III and IV.

— — Early Cartography of the Gulf of Mexico
and adjacent parts, [in No. 143, II, p. 217].
                                              R 232

— — The earliest Maps of the Portuguese and
Spanish Discoveries, [in No. 143, II, p. 93].
                                              R 233

Collected Voyages.

De Bry.

BARTLETT, J. R. Bibliographical Description of
a copy of De Bry. Providence : 1875. L 234

Also in No. 52, p. 316.

BOUCHER DE LA RICHARDERIE. *See* No. 151.

BRUNET, J. C. Notice Bibliographique sur la
Collection des Voyages de De Bry. Paris :
1860.   B 235

Also in the 5th edition of Manuel du Libraire, and a
translation by C. A. Cutter in Sabin's Dictionary (Vol.
V.) which was separately issued, " New York : 1869."

BURE, G. F. de. Voyages of De Bry, [in Bibliographie Instructive, p. 66]. Paris : 1768.
B 236

CAMUS, A. G. Memoire sur la Collection des Voyages [de De Bry] et sur la Collection des Voyages de Thevenot. Paris: 1802. B 237

COHN, A. Collection de De Bry, [in Catalogue de la Bibliotheque de S. Sobolewski, p. 240]. Leipzig : 1873. C 238

HUTH, Henry ? A Description and Collection of " De Bry's Voyages." London : 1880. L 239

Same in " The Huth Library," II, p. 404.

LINDSAY, L. Bibliotheca Lindesianana. Collections and Notes, No. 3. Grands et Petits Voyages de De Bry. London : 1884. C 240

MULLER, F. *See* No. 94.

PAYNE, J. T., and Foss, H. Description of the Voyages of De Bry, [in Bibliotheca Grenvilliana, I, p. 184]. London : 1842. L 241

[QUARITCH, B.] Collation of the German De Bry, First editions, [London: 1870]. 242

— — *See* No. 185.

ROTHELIN, C. d'Orléans de. Observations et details sur la collection des grands et petits voyages. [Paris :] 1742. B 243

·Also in Lenglet du Fresnoy's Méthode pour étudier la Geo., Paris : 1768, I, p. 324.

TIELE, P. A. *See* No. 190.

WEIGLE, T. O. Bibliographische Mittheilungen über die deutschen Ausgaben von De Bry's Sammlungen der Reisen. Leipzig : 1845.
B 244

Same in Naumann's Serapeum. 1845.

In No. 52 there is a list of all the important sets of De Bry sold from 1709 to 1875.

Hulsius.

ASHER, A. Bibliographical Essay on the Voyages and Travels, edited by Hulsius. London : 1839.   · B 245

BARTLETT, J. R. *See* No. 52.

[MOORE, G. H.] Contributions to a Catalogue of the Lenox Library, No. I. Voyages of Hulsius, etc. New York : 1877. L 246

TIELE, P. A. *See* No. 190.

Thevenot.

CAMUS, A. G. *See* No. 237.

MOORE, G. H. Contributions to a Catalogue of the Lenox Library, No. III. The Voyages of Thevenot. New York : 1879. L 247

ETHNOLOGY.

General Works.

TRÜBNER, N. *See* No. 137.

WAITZ, G. Literatur die Amerikaner Ethnographisch, [in Anthropologia der Naturvölker, III, p. xix]. Leipzig: 1872. R 248

Special Nations.

(Chinese.)

FOSTER, W. E. The Chinese in the U. S., [in Monthly Reference List, II, p. 11]. New York: 1882. R 249

GRIFFIN, A. P. C. The Chinese in America, [in Bost. Pub. Lib. Bull., IV, p. 143]. Boston: 1879.   R 250

(Dutch.)

ASHER, G. M. *See* Nos. 46 and 47.

JAMESON, J. F. *See* Individual—Usselinx.

MULLER, F. *See* Nos. 94 and 95.

TIELE, P. T. *See* Nos. 190 and 191.

(English.)

See Political Divisions.

EARLY English Explorations in America. *See* No. 162.

WINSOR, J. Chronological list of the earliest English books published on America, [in No. 143, III, p. 99].   B 251 ‡

(French.)

See Political Divisions, Canada.

CHARLEVOIX, P. F. X. de. *See* No. 61.

FARIBAULT, G. B. *See* No. 73.

(German.)

KÖRNER, G. Bibliography of the Germans in the United States, [in Das Deutsche Element in dem Vereinigten Staten]. Cincinnati: 1880.   R 252

SEIDENSTICKER, O. Deutsch-Americanische Bibliographie bis zum schlusse des letzten Jahrhunderts, [in Der Deutsche Pionier, VIII–XII].   B 253 ‡

(Indian.)

See also Philology, Indian.

No. 291 contains a Bibliography of Indian Bibliography.

BANCROFT, H. H. Authorities on the Indians, [in Native Races of the Pacific States, I, p. xvii]. New York: 1875.   B 254 *

CHASE, H. E. Bibliography of the Wampanoag Indians of Mass., [in Ann. Rep. of the Smithsonian Inst. for 1883, p. 906]. Washington: 1884.   B 255

DUNN, J. P. Authorities, [in Indian Wars of the far West, p. 757]. New York: 1886.   R 256

FIELD, THOMAS W. An Essay towards an Indian Bibliography. New York: 1873. B 257 *

— — *See* Sabin, J. No. 260.

INDIAN Tribes in the U. S., [in Month. Ref. Lists, III, p. 5]. New York: 1883.   R 258

KNAPP, A. M. Reference list on the Indian Question, [in Boston Pub. Lib. Bull., IV, p. 68]. Boston: 1878.   R 259

LIST of Authorities, [in some Account of the Conduct of the Religious Societies of Friends towards the Indian Tribes]. London: 1844.   R 259 (2)

LITTLEFIELD, G. E. Catalogues Nos. 8 and 10. Boston: 1882-3.   C 259 (3) *

[SABIN, JOSEPH.] Catalogue of the Library of Thomas W. Field. New York: 1875. A 260 *

SHEA, J. G. Authorities, [in Catholic Missions among the Indian Tribes, p. 503]. New York: 1855.   R 270

TRUMBULL, J. H. See No. 139.

WOODWARD, C. Catalogues No. XI and XVI.
New York: 1878; 1880.   C 271 *

(Italian.)

SAN FILIPO, P. A. de. See No. 179.

(Northmen.)

AUTHORITIES on America before Columbus, [in
Bost. Pub. Lib. Bull., III, p. 65]. Boston:
1877.   R 272

BROAM, M. A. Works on the Icelandic Discovery of America, [in Icelandic Discovery, p.
209]. London: 1887.   B 273

RAFN, Christiani. Conspectus codicum mem-
braneorum in quibus terraum Americanorum
mentio fit, [in Antiquitates Americanæ, p.
xxvii]. Hafniæ: 1837.   B 274

SLAFTER, E. S. Bibliography of the Northmen
in America, [in Voyages of the Northmen to
America, p. 127]. Boston: 1877.   B 275

WATSON, P. B. Bibliography of the Pre-Colum-
bian discovery of America, [in Library Journal, VI, p. 227]. New York: 1881.   B 276

WATSON, P. B. [Same, enlarged, in Anderson's
America not discovered by Columbus, 3d ed.,
p. 121]. Chicago: 1883.   B 277

(Spanish.)

See Political Divisions.

LEON PINELO, A. de. See Nos. 89–90.

MULLER, F. See No. 96.

NAVARETTE, M. F. See No. 173.

ROBERTSON, W. See No. 113.

WINSOR, J. Sources of early Spanish-American
History, [in No. 143, II, p. 1].   R 278

(Swedes.)

BIBLIOGRAPHIA Sueco Americana, [in Norton's
Literary Gazette, III, p. 216, and IV, p. 160].
New York : 1853–4.   B 279 ‡

PHILOLOGY.

General Works.

PLATZMANN, J. Verzeichniss einer Auswahl
Amerikanischer Grammatiken, Wörterbuch,
Katechismen, u. s. w. Leipzig : 1876.   B 281

QUARITCH, B. See Nos. 107 and 185.

TRÜBNER, N. See No. 137.

Americanisms.

BARTLETT, J. R. List of Authorities, [in Dictionary of Americanisms, p. xxix]. Boston :
1859.   R 282

TUCKER, G. M. Bibliography of American
English, [in American English]. Albany : 1883.
          R 283

Also in Trans. Albany Inst., p. 358.

Creole.

HEARN, L. Bibliography of the Creole Language, [in "Gumbo Zhèbes," p. 7]. New York:
1885.   B 283 (2)

Indian.

See Ethnology—Indian.

[BERENDT, C. H.] Los Trabajos Linguisticos de Juan Pio Perez. Merida: 1871. B 283 (2)

BRINTON, D. G. Aboriginal American Authors and their productions ; especially those in the native languages. Philadelphia : 1883. 284

— — Literature of the Cakchiquil language, [in Grammar of Cakchiquil Lang., p. 10]. Philadelphia : 1884. 285

CARRILLO Y ANCONA, D. C. Estudios Bibliograficos sobre la Historia de la Lengua Maya o Yucateca. [Mexico: 1872]. 285 (2)
Also in Bol. Soc. de Geog. Mex., 2 Series IV, p. 134.

CATALOGUE of books in the Astor Library relating to the Languages and Literature of Asia, Africa, and the Oceanic Islands. New York : 1864.
L 285 (3) |

GIBBS, G. Bibliography of the Chinook Jargon, [in Dictionary of the, p. xiii]. · Washington : 1863. B 286

— — Same, [in Alphabetical Vocabulary, p. vii). New York : 1863. B 287

ICAZBALCETA, J. G. Apuntes para un Catálogo de Escritores en Lenguas Indígenas de América. Mexico : 1866. 288

LECLERC, C. *See* No. 87.

LUDEWIG, H. E., and Turner, W. W. The Literature of American Aboriginal Languages. London: 1858. B 289 |

PILLING, J. C. Proof Sheets of a Bibliography of the Languages of the North American Indians. Washington: 1885. · B 291 *

PILLING, J. C. Bibliography of the Eskimo Language. Washington: 1887. B 292 *

· · — Bibliography of the Siouan Language. Washington: 1887. B 293 *

RIGGS, S. R. Bibliography of the Dakota Language, [in Grammar and Dictionary of the Dakota Language, p. xx]. Washington: 1853.
B 294

SCHOOLCRAFT, H. R. A Bibliographical Cat. of Books, Translations of the Scriptures, and other publications in the Indian Tongues of the U. S. Washington: 1849. B 295

— — Same, [in Indian Tribes, IV, p. 523]. Philadelphia: 1854. B 296

SOBRON, F. C. Y. Los Idiomas de la America Latina — Estúdios Biografico-Bibliograficos. Madrid: 1879. B 297

SQUIER, E. G. Monograph of authors who have written on the Languages of Central America. New York: 1861. B 298

TRÜBNER, N. *See* No. 137.

— — A Catalogue of works on the Aboriginal Languages of America. London: 1874.
C 300 |

— — Catalogue of Dictionaries and Grammars. London: 1882. C 300 (2) |
Earlier edition, London : 1872.

TRUMBULL, J. H. *See* No. 139.

— — Origin ... of Indian Missions in New England with a list of books in the Indian Language printed at Cambridge and Boston, 1653–1721. Worcester: 1874. B 299 ‡
Same in Proceedings of the Am. Antiq. Soc.

ZOÖLOGY.

Classed under
>   General Works.
>   Anthropology.
>   Mammalogy.
>   Ornithology.
>   Herpetology.
>   Ichthyology.
>   Entomology.
>   Crustaceology.
>   Molluscology.
>   Conchology.
>   For writings of Scientists, *see* Individual.

General Works.

AGASSIZ, L., and Strickland, H. E. Bibliographia Zoologiæ et Geologiæ. London : 1848–54.
B 301

CATALOGUE of the Publications of the U. S. Geological and Geographical Survey of the Territories. Third Edition. Washington : 1879.
302
There are earlier editions, 1874 ; 1877, and a later one in Ex. Doc., No. 182, 47th Cong., 1st session, Senate.

GILL, T. Bibliography of Zoölogy, 1882, [in Rep. of the Smithsonian Inst. for 1882]. Washington : 1883. B 303

— — Bibliography of Zoölogy, 1883, [in Rep. of the Smithsonian Inst. for 1883]. Washington: 1884. B 304

GIRARD, C. Bibliographia Americana Historico-Naturalis, for 1851. Washington : 1852.
B 305
Also in Am. Journal of Science and Art, XII, p. 1.

KINGSLEY, J. S. Bibliography of Zoölogy, [in Naturalist's Assistant, p. 145]. Boston : 1882.
B 305a

MURDOCH, J. Bibliography of the Marine Invertebrates of Alaska, [in Rep. of the Inter. Polar Ex. to Point Barrow, p. 136]. Washington : 1885. B 306

ORBIGNY, A. d'. Catalogue de livres d'histoire naturelle. Ouvrages et manuscrits relatifs à l'Amérique. Paris : 1858. B 307

Anthropology.

BOEMER, G. H. Index to papers on Anthropology pub. by the Smithsonian Inst. 1847–1878. Washington : 1881. B 308
Also in Rep. of the Regents of the Smithsonian Institution for 1878.

MASON, O. T. Bibliography of Anthropology, [in Rep. of the Regents of the Smithsonian Inst. for 1880]. Washington : 1881. B 309

WAITZ, T. Literature of American Anthropology, [in Anthropologie der Naturvölker, III]. Leipzig : 1872. B 310

Mammalogy.

GILL, T. Bibliography of Mammals, [in Arrangement of the Families of Mammals]. Washington : 1872. B 311

Also in Smithsonian Misc. Coll., XI.

— — and Coues, E. Materials for a Bibliography of North American Mammals. Washington : 1877. B 312

Also in U. S. Geological Survey of the Territories, XI, p. 951.

Ornithology.

COUES, E. Bibliography of American Ornithology, [in Birds of the North West. Miscellaneous pub. U. S. Geo. Sur., No. 3]. Washington: 1874. B 313

— — Bibliography of American Ornithology, [in Bull. U. S. Geolog. and Geograph. Survey, No. 6]. Washington: 1876. B 314

— — List of faunal publications relative to N. A. Ornithology, [in Birds of the Colorado Valley, p. 567]. Washington: 1878. B 315

Herpetology.

LOCKINGTON, W. N. Review of the progress of North American batrachology, 1880–83, [in Am. Naturalist, XVIII, p. 149]. 316

MITCHELL, S. W. Bibliography of Venomous Snakes, [in Researches on Venomous Snakes]. Washington: 1860. B 317

Also in Smithsonian Contrib. to Knowledge, XII.

Ichthyology.

BEAN, T. H. A partial Bibliography of the fishes of the Pacific Coast of the U. S. and Alaska, for 1880, [in Pro. of the U. S. Nat. Mus, for 1881]. Washington: 1882. B 318

GILL, T. Bibliography of Fishes, [in Arrangement of the Families of Fishes]. Washington: 1872. B 319

Also in Smithsonian Misc. Coll., XI.

— — Bibliography of the Fishes of the Pacific Coast of the U. S. Washington: 1882. B 320

Also in the Smithsonian Misc. Coll., XXIII.

SMILEY, C. W. List of published reports of the Fishery Commissioners of the various States of the U. S., [in Bull. U. S. Fish Comm., III, p. 85]. Washington: 1884. B 321

Entomology.

MAN, B. P. Bibliography of some of the literature concerning destructive insects, [in Second Rep. of the U. S. Entomological Commission]. Washington: 1881. B 322

PACKARD, A. S. Bibliography of the Geometrid Moths of the U. S., [in U. S. Geological Survey of the Territories, X, p. 595]. Washington: 1876. B 323

SACKEN, C. R. O. Bibliography of Diptera, [in Catalogue of the Described Diptera]. Washington: 1878.   B 324
Also in Smithsonian Misc. Coll., XVI.

SCUDDER, S. H. Bibliography of Orthoptera [in Cat. of the Orthoptera of N. A.]. Washington: 1868.   B 325
Also in Smithsonian Misc. Coll., VIII.

Crustaceology.

HUXLEY, T. H. Bibliography, [in The Crayfish]. New York: 1881.   B 326

Molluscology.

GILL, T. Bibliography of Mollusks, [in Arrangement of the Families of Mollusks]. Washington: 1871.   B 327
Also in Smithsonian Misc. Coll., X.

Conchology.

BINNEY, W. G. Bibliography of N. A. Conchology. 2 Parts. Washington: 1863-4.   B 328
Also in Smithsonian Miscell. Coll., V. and IX.

TRYON, G. W. American writers on recent Conchology. New York: 1861.   329

WOODWARD, A. Bibliography of recent and fossil Foraminifera, [in Min. Geological and Natural History Survey, Annual Report, part 5]. St. Paul: 1885.   B 330

BOTANY.

General Works.

WATSON, S. Bibliographical Index to North American Botany. Washington: 1878. B 331

Special Work.

FARLOW, W. G., and Trelease, W. List of Works on North American Fungi. Cambridge: 1887.   B 332

UNDERWOOD, L. M. D. Bibliography of North American Hepaticæ, [in Bull. Ill. State Lab. of Nat. Hist. II, p. 15]. Chicago: 1884.   B 333

WOOD, H. C. Bibliography of Algæ. [in Hist. of Fresh-Water Algæ of N. A.]. Washington: 1872.   B 334
Also in Smithsonian Collections, XIX.

MINERALOGY.

Classed under
    General Works.
    Geology.
    Palæontology.
    Earthquakes.

General Works.

LIS , R. Classified Index to the Maps in the Publications of the Geological Society of London, 1811-1885, Boston: 1887.   R 335
Also in Bull. Boston Pub. Lib.

DANA, E. S. Bibliography of Mineralogy, [in Ann. Rep. of the Smithsonian Inst. for 1883, p, 676]. Washington: 1884.   B 336

DAWSON, J. W. D.   Bibliography, [in Arcadian Geology, p. 8].   London: 1868.   B 337

Geology.

LESLIE, J. P.   List of the publications of the Second Geological Survey of Pennsylvania, [in Historical Sketch, XXII].   Harrisburg: 1876.
          B 338

— — Sketch of the Literature of Geology in the United States, [in Historical Sketch of the Second Geo. Survey of Pa., p. 4].   Harrisburg: 1876.   339

LIST of reports and maps of the U. S. geographical Surveys west of the 100th Meridian.   Washington: 1882.   340

Earlier edition, 1878.

MAFFEI, E., and Figueron, R. R.   Apuntes para una biblioteca española relativos al conocimiento y explotacion de las riquezas minerales y geología.   Madrid: 1872.   341

MERRILL, F. J. H.   Index of current Literature relating to American Geology, [in School of Mines Quarterly].   New York: Jan. 1887. 342

MARCOU, J.   Books on North American Geology, [in A Geological Map of the U. S., p. 89].   Boston: 1853.   B 343

— — List of Authorities on North American Geology, [in Bul. de la Soc. Geologique, II, 930].   Paris: 1863.   344

— — Mapotica Geologica Americana, 1752-1881.   Washington: 1884.   345

— — List of Maps and Memoirs on the geology of North America, [in Geology of N. A., p. 122].   Zurich: 1858.   346

[MARSH, O. C.]   A Catalogue of Official Reports upon Geological Surveys of the United States and British Provinces.   n. p. 1867.
          B 347

Also in Am Jour. of Sci. and Arts, XLII, p. 116.

PRIME, F., Jr.   A Catalogue of Official Reports upon Geological Surveys of the U. S. and British North America.   Philadelphia: 1879.
          B 348

Also in Trans. of the Am. Inst. of Mining Engineers, VII, p. 255.

SELWYN, A. R. C.   List of Publications of the Geological Survey of Canada.   Montreal: 1873.
          B 349

SWALLOW, G. C.   Works on Missouri Geology, [in Geol. Survey of Mo., I and II Reports, p. 209].   Jefferson City: 1855.   B 350

THOMASSY, R.   See No. 220.

WHEELER, G. M.   List of works on topographic and geological survey operations, [in Rep. on the 3d International Geog. Congress, p. 539].   351

WHITNEY, J. D.   List of American Authors in Geology and Palæontology.   Cambridge: 1882.
          352

Palæontology.

MARCOU, J. B.   Review of the progress of N. A. Palæontology for 1883.   Washington: 1884.
          R 353

MARCOU, J. B.   Same for 1884.   Washington:
    1885.   R 354
— — Same for 1884-5, [in American Naturalist,
    XIX, p. 853, and XX, p. 505].   1885.   R 355
— — Bibliography of publications relative to the
    collection of fossil insects in the U. S. Nat.
    Museum, including complete lists of the writ-
    ings of F. B. Meek, C. A. White, and C. D.
    Walcott.   Washington: 1885.   B 356
SCUDDER, S. H.   A Bibliography of Fossil In-
    sects.   Cambridge: 1882.   B 357
WHITE, C. A., and Nicholson, H. A.   Bibliog-
    raphy of N. A. invertebrate palæontology.
    Washington: 1878.   B 358
WHITNEY.   See No. 352.

Earthquakes.

MILNE, J.   Authorities on Earthquakes, [in
    Earthquakes and other Earth Movements, p.
    349].   New York: 1886.   359
POEY, A.   Bibliography relative to Earthquakes
    in the Western World, [in Annuaire de la
    société météorologique de France, V, 245].
    Paris: 1857.   B 360

HISTORY.

See also America—general. Political Divisions.
ADAMS, C. K.   American Works, [in a Manual of
    Historical Literature].   New York: 1882.
                                              B 361
FOSTER, W. E.   Reference list on the Founda-
    tion of the American Colonies, [in Library
    Journal, V, p. 329].   New York : 1880.   R 362
MARSH, E. G.   A supplement to Dr. Priestly's
    lectures on history, exhibiting a series of
    American Histories.   New Haven: 1801.
                                              R 363
SPARKS, J.   List of works on American History,
    [in W. Smith's Lectures on modern History].
    Cambridge: 1841.   B 364

JURISPRUDENCE.

AMIAUD, A.   Statute Laws of America, [in
    Aperçu de l'état actuel des legislations civiles].
    Paris: 1884.   365
BAKER, Voorhis & Co.   Catalogue of Law Books.
    New York: 1881.   C 366
BATES, C.   Digest of Law Publications.   Cin-
    cinnati: 1886.   C 367
CAREY, M.   Catalogue of Law Books for sale.
    Philadelphia: 1820.   C 368
CLARKE, R.   Digest of American and British
    Law publications.   Cincinnati: 1877.
                                          C 369 | *
— — Short title list of Law Books.   Cincinnati:
    1887.   C 370 * |
CONGRESS.   Catalogue of Books in the Law De-
    partment of the Library of Congress.   Wash-
    ington: 1839.   L 371
— Laws of the U. S., and of the several States,
    [in Catalogue of the Library of, p. 162].   Wash-
    ington: 1830.   L 372
DEPARTMENT of State.   Law books in, [in Cata-
    logue of the Library of].   Washington: 1830.
                                              L 373

De Witt, W. Law Books. [in Catalogue of the Pa. States Library]. Harrisburg: 1859. L 374

Dietz, A. P. Works on American Law, [in Bibliotheca Californica]. Sacramento: 1870.
L 375

Gould, W. Catalogue of Law Books. Albany: 1881. C 376

Griffith, W. Catalogue of law books and statute laws published in each State and the United States, [in Annual Law Register of the U. S., Vols. 3 and 4]. Burlington, N. J.: 1822.
B 377

Guernsey, R. S. Bibliography of Legal Bibliography. New York: 1874. B 378 ‡

Harvard University. Catalogue of the Dana Law Library of. Cambridge: 1841. L 379
See also Sumner.

Johnson, T. and J. W. Catalogue of Law Books. Philadelphia: 1847. C 380

Kay, — ? Catalogue of Law Books. Philadelphia: 1854. C 381

Lewis & Blood's General Catalogue of Law Books. New York: 1853. C 382

Little & Brown's Catalogue of Law Books. Boston: 1843. C 383

Marvin, J. G. Legal Bibliography. Philadelphia: 1847. B 384

— — Same. Philadelphia. 1883. B 385

Parsons, J. D., Jr. Catalogue of Law Books. Albany: 1884. C 386

Randolph, J. W. Catalogue of Law Books. Richmond: 185-. C 387

Roorback, O. A. American Law books, [in Bibliotheca Americana, 1820–1848, p. 321]. New York: 1849. B 388

New York State Library. Catalogue of the Law Library of. Albany: 1856. L 389

— — Same, Supplement. Albany: 1865. L 390

— — Same, Subject Index to. Albany: 1882.
L 391

Shinn, C. H. Authorities, [in Land Laws of Mining Districts, Johns Hopkins University Studies. 2 series, XII]. Baltimore: 1884.
R 392

[Sumner, C.] Catalogue of the Law Library of Harvard College. Cambridge: 1837. L 393

Vanderpoel, A. J. Catalogue of the books in the Library of the New York Law Institute New York: 1874. L 394 * †

LITERATURE.

See America—General Works. Political Divisions.

PHILOSOPHY.

Philosophy in America, [in Prov. Ref. List. III, p. 12]. New York: 1883. R 395

THEOLOGY.

Classed under
General Works.
The Bible.
Sects and Beliefs.

General Works.

Bibliography of Theological Bibliography, [in No. 401, p. 375]. Princeton: 1886.   396

HURST, J. F. Bibliotheca Theologica. New York: 1883.   C 397

LAURIE, T. List of works published by the missions and missionaries of the American Board of Commissioners of Foreign Missions, [in The Ely Volume, p. 485]. N. Y.: 1886.   398

MACCLINTOCK, J., and Strong, J. Cyclopædia of Theological and Ecclesiastical Literature. New York: 1867-187-.   399

MALCOLM, H. References to the principal works in every department of Religious Literature. Boston: 1868.   R 400

PRINCETON Theological School. Catalogue of the library of. Pt. I. Religious Literature. Princeton: 1866.   L 401

The Bible.

HALL, Isaac H. Bibliography of the Greek New Testament as published in America. Philadelphia: 1883.   B 402 |

O'CALLAGHAN, E. B. List of Editions of the Holy Scriptures printed in America previous to 1860. Albany: 1861.   B 403 |

SHEA, J. G. Bibliographical Account of Catholic Bibles, etc., printed in the United States. New York: 1859.   B 404 |

Sects.

(Baptists.)

HAYNES, T. W. Baptist Cyclopædia, or Dictionary of Baptist Biography, Bibliography, etc. Charleston: 1848.   B 406

(Catholics.)

See Jesuits.

FIOTTI, J. M. Bibliographia Catholica Americana. New York: 1872.   B 407 *

— —Catalogue of the Library of. New York: 1879.   A 408 *

(Congregational.)

See also Political Divisions—New England.

DEXTER, Henry Martin. Collections towards a Bibliography of Congregationalism, [in Congregationalism as seen in its Literature]. New York: 1880.   B 409 |

(Episcopal.)

List of Bishops, Deans, etc., who have preached before the Society for the Propagation of the Gospel in Foreign Parts, [in Ann. Sermon: for 1785]. London: 1785.   R 410 |
A more perfect list in No. 52, III, p. 271.

(Jesuits.)

See also Political Divisions—Canada.

BACKER, A. de. Bibliothèque des écrivains de la Compagnie de Jésus. Paris: 1869-1876.   B 411

BIBLIOGRAPHY of Jesuitism, [in Lit. World, XIV, p. 132]. Boston: 1882.   R 412

CARAYON, A. Bibliographie historique de la Compagnie de Jésus. Paris: 1864.   B 413

MURATORI. *See* No. 889.

RIBADENEIRA, P., and Algambe, P. Bibliotheca scriptorum Societatis Iesu. Romæ: 1676.

B 414

(Lutherans.)

MORRIS, J. G. Bibliotheca Lutherana; A complete list of publications of all the Lutheran Ministers in the United States. Philadelphia: 1876.   415

(Methodists.)

[CAVENDER, H. C.] Catalogue of Works in refutation of Methodism. New York: 1868.

B 416 *

Earlier edition, Philadelphia: 1846.

OSBORN, G. Outlines of Wesleyan Bibliography; or, a record of Methodist Literature. London: 1869.   417

(Moravians.)

MALIN, Wm. G. Catalogue of books relating to or illustrating the history of the Unitas Fratum ... generally known as the Moravian Church. Philadelphia: 1881.   B 418

SCHWEINITZ, E. de. Literature relating to the Unitas Fratum, [in History of the, p. vii]. 1885.

B 419

(Mormons.)

BURTON, R. F. List of works upon the subject of Mormonism, [in The City of the Saints, p. 203]. New York: 1862.   B 420

REMY, J. Bibliographie Mormonne, [in Voyage au pays des Mormons, II, 499]. Paris: 1860.

B 421

Also in English edition, London: 1861.

STENHOUSE, T. B. H. Writers on Mormonism, [in The Rocky Mountain Saints, p. 741]. New York: 1873.   B 422

WOODWARD, C. L. Bibliotheca Scallawagiana. Catalogue of Books relating to Mormonism. New York: 1880.   A 423 *

(Native.)

MÜLLER, J. G. Authorities, [in Geschichte der Americanischen Ur-religionen]. Basel: 1855.

424

(Perfectionists.)

NORDHOFF, C. Bibliography of the Oneida Community, [in Communistic Societies of the U. S., p. 428]. New York: 1875.   B 425 |

(Quakers.)

LIST of Authorities, [in Some Account of the Conduct of the Religious Society of Friends towards the Indian Tribes]. London: 1844.

R 426

SMITH, J. Descriptive Catalogue of Friends Books. London: 1867.   B 427 *

— — Bibliotheca Anti-Quakeriana. London: 1873.   B 428 *

— — Bibliotheca Quakeristica. A bibliography of miscellaneous literature relating to Friends. Part I. London: 1883.   429

— — Catalogue of Books and Pamphlets of the Society of Friends. London [n. d.]   C 430 *

— — Catalogue of Books relating to the Society of Friends. London [n. d.]   C 431 *

(Shakers.)

NORDHOFF, C. Bibliography of the Shakers, [in Communistic Societies of the U. S., p. 421]. New York, 1875. B 432 |

(Unitarians.)

GILLETT, E. H. Bibliography of the Unitarian Controversy, [in Historical Magazine, XIX, 316]. Morrisania: 1871. B 433 |

(Universalists.)

EDDY, R. Bibliography, [in Universalism in America, p. 485]. Boston: 1886. B 434

POLITICAL DIVISIONS.

Newfoundland.

BONNYCASTLE, R. H. List of works on Newfoundland, [in Newfoundland in 1842]. London: 1842. 435

SWEETZER, M. F. *See* No. 452.

Canada.

Classed under

General Works.

Jesuit Relations.

See also U. S., Military History.

(General Works.)

BANCROFT, H. H. Authorities on British Columbia, [in Hist. of the Pacific States, XXVII, p. 23]. San Francisco: 1887. B 437 *

BRYCE, G. List of Works, [in Manitoba: its infancy, growth, and present condition, p. 365]. London, 1882. P 438

CATALOGUE. *See* Nos. 59 and 60.

CHARLEVOIX, P. F. X. de. *See* No. 61.

COATS, W. Works on Hudsons Bay, [in The Geography of Hudsons Bay]. London: 1852. B 439

DAVIS, A. M. Sources of information relative to Canada and Louisiana, [in No. 143, V., p. 63]. R 440

DAWSON, J. W. D. *See* No. 337.

DE COSTA, B. F. Sources of information relative to Jacques Cartier and his successors, [in No. 143, IV, p. 62]. R 441

FARIBAULT, G. B. *See* No. 73.

FERRARIO, J. List of books on the North East, North West, and Canada, [in No. 74(1), pp. 77, 145, and 241]. B 442

GAGNON, P. Catalogues 1 to 10. Quebec: 1885-1888. C 443 *

[HARRISSE, H.] Notes pour servir à l'Histoire, à la Bibliographie et à la Cartographie de la Nouvelle-France. Paris: 1872. B 445 |

LAET, J. de. Works on Nova Francia, [in No. 84].

LIST of works on Canada, [in Mémoires Justificats des Commissaires, IV, 539]. Paris: 1857. R 446

MARCEL. *See* No. 210.

MEIKLE. *See* No. 605.

MORGAN, H. J. Bibliotheca Canadensis. Ottawa: 1867. B 447 *

MURDOCH, B. Authorities, [in History of Nova Scotia, or Arcadie, I, p. 533]. Halifax: 1865. B 448

PIDDINGTON, A. Catalogue Seven. Bibliotheca Canadensis. Toronto: 1884.   C 449

REFERENCE list on Canada, [in Monthly Ref. List, IV, p. 19]. New York: 1884.   R 449 (2)

SELWYN, A. R. C. *See* No. 349.

SHEA, J. G. *See* No. 270.

SMITH, C. C. Sources of information relative to Arcadia, [in No. 143, IV, p. 149].   R 450

STEWART, G., Jr. Sources of information relative to Frontenac and the history of New France, [in No. 143, IV, p. 354].   R 451

SWEETSER, M. F. Authorities on the Maritime Provinces of Canada, [The Maritime Prov., p. 334]. Boston: 1875.   B 452

WATSON, J. M. Canada, [in Catalogue of the Library of Parliament, p. 77]. Toronto: 1881.   L 453

WINSOR, J. *See* Nos. 225 (2) to 229.

Jesuit Relations. *See* also Theology.

BARTLETT, J. R. *See* No. 35.

[MOORE, G. H.] Jesuit Relations. Contributions to a Catalogue of the Lenox Library. No. II. The Jesuit Relations, etc. New York: 1879.   L 454 |

NASH, E. *See* No. 52.

O'CALLAGHAN, E. B. Catalogue of Jesuit Relations. New York: 1847.   R 455 |
Also in Pro. of the N. Y. Hist. Soc. for 1847, and an edition translated into French. Montreal: 1850.

— — A few notes on the Jesuit Relations. [New York:] 1853.   R 456 |

SHEA, J. G. Sources of information relative to the Jesuits in America, [in No. 143, IV, p. 263].   R 457

WINSOR, J. Jesuit Relations, [in No. 143, IV, p. 295].   B 458 |

United States.
Classed under
    Geography.
    History.
    Literature.
    Local Divisions.

(Geography.)
See also America, in general. Geography.

BARTLETT, J. R. Bibliography of Carver's Travels, [in Bookmart, IV, p. 17]. Pittsburg: 1886.   B 459

COUES, E. Publications relating to Lewis and Clarke's travels, [in Bull. of the U. S. Geol. and Geog. Survey, No. 6, p. 417]. Washington: 1876.   B 460

TUCKERMAN, H. T. America, and her Commentators. New York: 1864.   R 461 |

(History.)
Classed under
    General.
    Military.
    Civil.
    See also America, in general. History.

General History.

BUTLER, F. Authorities, [in Complete History of the U. S., III, p. 460]. Hartford: 1821.
R 462

HANDELMANN, H. Authorities, [in Geschichte de Amerikanischen Kolonisation]. Kiel: 1856.
463

HART, A. B. List of Readings on the History of the U. S., [in Academy, II, 158, 367]. Syracuse: May, 1887.
R 465

HILDRETH, R. Authorities, [in History of the U. S., III and VI]. New York: 1849.
B 466

[MUNSELL, F.]. A Classified Catalogue of the American Historical Publications of the Munsell Press. [Albany: 1883.]
C 467

ROBINSON, T. A. L. List of sources of the historical origin of the U. S., [in Geschichte der Colonization in Neu England]. von Talvi, Leipzig: 1847.
468
Also in London ed. 1851.

SAGRA, R. de la. Authorities, [in Cinco Mens los Estados-Unidos, p. xxvii]. Paris: 1836.
469

Military History—French and Indian War.

HALE, E. E. See No. 204.

WINSOR, J. Sources of information relative to the French and Indian War, [in No. 143, V, pp. 420 and 560].
R 470

Military History—Revolution.

CENTENNIAL Readings. Literature of 1776, [in Bost. Pub. Lib. Bull., III].
R 471

DRAKE, F. S. Bibliography of the Society of the Cincinnati, [in Memorials, p. 537]. Boston: 1873.
B 472

FRENCH Allies. [In Monthly Ref. List, 11]. New York: 1881.
R 473

HAVEN and Thomas. See No. 557.

HILDEBURN, C. R. See No. 577.

LEXINGTON, Concord, and Bunker Hill, [in Bull. Bost. Pub. Lib., II, 350].
R 474

LIST of works relating to Bancroft's History of the Revolution, [in Mag. of Am. Hist., VIII, p. 706]. New York: 1882.
B 475

LITERATURE of the Revolution, [in Bost. Pub. Lib. Bull., III, p. 31 and 172].
R 476

LITERATURE of the History of Boston during the Revolution, [in Bost. Pub. Lib. Bull., II, p. 382].
R 477

SMITH, L. P. Bibliography of the Society of the Cincinnati. Philadelphia: 1885.
B 478
Also in Bull. Lib. Co. of Phila.

SOURCES of information relative to the Revolutionary War, [in No. 143, VI].
R 479

STEVENS, B. F. Bibliography of the Clinton-Cornwallis controversy, [in The Campaign in Virginia, 1781, I]. London: 1888.
B 480

STOCKBRIDGE, J. C. Pamphlets relating to the Revolutionary War, [in Mag. of Am. Hist., VII, p. 310]. New York: 1881.
480 (2)

STONE, E. M. Works relating to the Invasion [in 1775] of Canada, [in Journal of Captain Simeon Thayer, p. iv]. Providence: 1867.
B 481

TREATY of Peace, 1783, [in Monthly Ref. List,
III, p. 30]. New York: 1883.   R 482
TRUMBULL, J. H. *See* No. 139.
WINSOR, J. List of diaries of Arnold's Expedi-
tion to Canada, [in Diary of Eben. Wild].
Cambridge: 1886.   483
— — Readers' Handbook of the American Revo-
lution 1761–1783. Boston.   R 484
WOODWARD, C. L. Catalogue of tidbits relat-
ing to the American Revolution. New York:
1877.   C 485
YORKTOWN. Reference List on, [in Monthly
Ref. List., I, 10]. New York: 1881.· R 486

Military History—Rebellion.

ABBOTT, G. M. Contributions towards a Bibliography of the Civil War. I, Regimental Histo-
ries. Philadelphia: 1886.   B 487 |
ANGLIM, J. Catalogue of Books and Pamphlets
relating to the late Civil War. Washington:
1882.   C 488 *
— — Catalogue of Books and Pamphlets on the
Civil War. Washington: 1886.   C 489
BARTLETT, J. R. The Literature of the Rebellion. Boston: 1866.   B 490 *
CATALOGUE of books on the Rebellion in the
library of the Wisconsin Hist. Soc. Madison:
1887.   L 491
CLARKE, R. List of Books and Pamphlets on
the Rebellion. Cincinnati: 1886.   C 492
[GRANT, S. H.] Bibliography of the Civil War,
[in Hist. Mag., VI, pp. 113, 146, 186, 206, 245,
342, VII, p. 112, and in Am. Publish. Circular,
I, 213]. New York and Philadelphia : 1862–3.
                                      R 493
TREADWELL, D. M. Catalogue of Books and
Pamphlets relating to the Civil War. Brooklyn: 1874.   B 494 *

Civil History.

Classed under
    General Works.
    Presidential Administrations.
    Political Questions.

General Works.

JOHNSTON, A. Bibliography of American Politics, [in Am. Politics, p. viii]. New York:
1885.   B 495

Presidential Administrations.

FOSTER, W. E. Reference List to Presidential
Administration, [in Economic Tracts, 17].
New York: 1885.   R 496†
WASHINGTON, [in Monthly Ref. List, I and III]
                                      R 496 (2)
ADAMS, J., [in Monthly Ref. List. I].   R 497
JEFFERSON, ["   "   "   " III]. R 498
— *See* Individual.
MADISON, [in Monthly Ref. List, III].   R 499
MONROE, ["   "   "   "   "]. R 500
— *See* Individual.
ADAMS, J. Q., [in Monthly Ref. List, III].
                                      R 500 (2)
JACKSON, [in Monthly Ref. List, IV].   R 501
— *See* Individual.
VAN BUREN, [in Monthly Ref. List, IV]. R 502

HARRISON and Tyler, [in Monthly Ref. List, IV]
R 503
— *See* Individual.
POLK, [in Monthly Ref. List, IV]. R 505
TAYLOR and Fillmore, [in Monthly Ref. List, IV].
R 506
BUCHANAN, [in Monthly Ref. List, IV]. 506(2)
FROM 1861 to 1885, [in Literary News, VI, pp. 82, 114, 146]. New York: 1886. R 507

Political Questions.
Classed under
Constitutional and Governmental.
Revenue and Finance,
Commerce and Navigation.
Foreign Questions.
Race Questions.

Constitutional and Governmental.
See also Jurisprudence.

BARNWELL, J. G. Reading Notes on the Constitution of the U. S., [Bull. Lib. Co. of Phila., July–Sept., p. 48]. Philadelphia: 1887. R 508
CATALOGUE of works relating to political economy and the science of government in the Library of Congress. Arranged by subject. Washington: 1869. L 509
CIVIL Service, [in Monthly Ref., III]. R 510
DAWSON, H. B. Bibliography of the Federalist, [in The Federalist]. New York: 1863.
B 511 |
DUNNING, W. A. Authorities, [in the Constitution of the U. S. in Civil War and Reconstruction, 1860–1867]. New York: 1885. R 512
ELECTIVE Judiciary, [in Monthly Ref. List, III].
R 513
FORD, P. L. A List of Editions of " The Federalist." Brooklyn: 1886. B 514 ‡
FOSTER, W. E. Reference list on the U. S. Constitution, [in Lib. Journal, V, pp. 172 and 222]. New York: 1880. R 515 †
— — The Literature of Civil Service Reform in the U. S. Providence: 1881. R 516
LOCAL Self-Government, [in Monthly Ref. List, II]. R 517
LODGE, H. C. Bibliography of the Federalist, [in Hamilton's Works, IX]. New York: 1887.
R 518
MEAD, E. D. The Constitution of the U. S. with Bibliographical Notes. Boston: 1887.
B 519
SALMON, L. M. List of Authorities on the Appointing power of the President, [in Papers of the Am. Hist. Ass., I, 414]. New York: 1886.
R 520
SHINN, C. H. Authorities on American Frontier Government, [in Mining Camps, p. 299]. New York: 1885. R 521
WEBSTER and the Constitution, [in Monthly Ref. List, II]. R 522

Revenue and Finance.

BOURNE, E. G. Bibliographic Index, [in The Surplus Revenue of 1837, p. 151]. New York: 1885. R 523

LAUGHLIN, J. L. Brief Bibliography of the Tariffs of the U. S., [in Mill's Principles of Political Economy, p. 631]. Boston: 1885. B 524

—— Brief Bibliography of Bi-metallism, [in Mill's Principles of Political Econ.]. New York: 1885. B 525

NATIONAL Banks, [in Monthly Ref. List, II]. R 526

PAINE, N. Books in the American Antiquarian Soc. which refer to Colonial or Continental Paper Money, [in Remarks on the early paper currency of Mass., p. 63]. Cambridge: 1866. R 527 ‡

Also in Proc. Am. Antiq. Soc. for 1866.

TARIFF Legislation in the U. S., [in Monthly Ref. List., II]. R 528

TAUSSIG, F. W. Authorities on the U. S. Tariff, 1860–1883, [in History of the present Tariff, p. ix]. New York: 1885. R 529

Commerce and Navigation.

FISHERIES. See No. 56.

FREE Ships, [in Monthly Ref. List, I]. R 530

FRENCH Spoliations. List of Works on, [in Bull. Boston Pub. Library, VI, p. 393]. R 531

LAUGHLIN, J. L. Bibliography of American Shipping, [in Mill's Principles of Pol. Econ., p. 635]. New York: 1885. B 532

PREBLE, G. H. Bibliography, [in Chronological History and Development of Steam Navigation, p. 414]. Philadelphia: 1883. B 533

Foreign Questions.

DWIGHT, T. F. Catalogue of the works relative to the law of nations and diplomacy in the library of the Department of State. Washington: 1886. L 534

FRENCH Spoliations. See No. 531.

JAMESON, J. F. Bibliography of the Monroe doctrine, [in Gilman's Life of James Monroe]. Boston: 1883. B 535

Race Questions.

CHINESE Question. See Nos. 249 and 250.

INDIAN Question. See Ethnology.

Negro.

See also Military History—Rebellion.

ANTI-SLAVERY periodicals in the May Collection of the Cornell Library. Cornell Library, I, 229. B 536

ALEXANDER, G. W. List of Authorities, [in Letters on the Slave Trade, etc.]. London: 1842. R 537

LIST of works on [pro] Slavery, [in Report and Treatise on Slavery and the Slavery Agitation]. Austin : 1857. B 538

LITERATURE.

Classed under

General Works.
Government Publications.
Imprints.
Periodicals.
Poetry.
Miscellaneous.

See also all Classes.

General Works.

ADAMS, O. F. Brief Handbook of American Authors. Boston: 1884. R 539

ALLIBONE. *See* No. 44.

AMERICAN Catalogue of Books, giving the full title of original works published in the U. S. since 1800 to 1855. London: 1856. R 540

ANNUAL American Catalogue for 1886. New York: 1887. B 541

— — for 1887. New York: 1888. B 542

BLAKE, A. V. The American Booksellers' Reference trade list. Claremont, N. H.: 1847. B 543

BOWKER, R. R., and Appleton, A. I. The American Catalogue. 1876-1884. New York: 1885. B 543 (2) * †

BUTLER, J. D. American Pre-Revolutionary *Bibliography. Andover: 1879. 544
Also in Bib. Sacra, January, 1879.

CATALOGUE of all the Books printed in the United States. Boston: 1804. B 545

DUYCKINCK, E. A. and G. L. Cyclopedia of American Literature. New York: 1856. R 546

HAVEN. *See* No. 557.

KELLY, J. The American Catalogue of Books. 1861-1866. New York: 1866.
— — Vol. II. 1866-1871. New York: 1871. B 547 *

LEON. Catalogue of first Editions of American Authors. C 550 *

LEYPOLDT, F. The American Catalogue of Books for 1869. New York: 1870. B 551

— — Annual Catalogue for 1870, [in Trade Circular Ann.]. New York: 1871. B 552

— — The Annual American Catalogue. Books published in the U. S., 1871. New York: 1872. B 553

— — and Jones, L. E. The American Catalogue of books in print and for sale, July 1, 1876. New York: 1880. B 553 * †

REUSE, J. D. Alphabetical Register of all Authors living in Great Britain, Ireland, and the United Provinces of North America, with a catalogue of their publications from 1770 to [1803]. Berlin: 1804. 553

ROORBACH, O. A. Bibliotheca Americana. Catalogue of American publications from 1820 to 1852. New York: 1852. B 554 *

— — Supplement, 1852 to 1855. New York: 1855. B 555 *

— — Addenda, 1855-1858. New York: 1858. B 556 *

— — Supplement, 1858-1861. New York: 1861. B 556 (2) *

SABIN. *See* No. 114.

THOMAS, I., and Haven, S. F. Catalogue of publications in the U. S., 1639-1775. Albany: 1874. B 557 ‡

TRÜBNER. *See* No. 137.

Government Publications.

ANGLIM, J. List of Books published by the Department of the Interior. Washington: 1881. C 558

— — — List of publications issued by Congress and

the Executive Department, from 1867 to 1881.
Washington: 1881.   C 559

ANGLIM, J. Monthly Bulletin of the Publications
of the U. S. Government. Nos. 1-17. Washington: 1883-8.   C 560

— — List of the publications of the U. S. Government on Fish and Fisheries. Washington:
1883.   C 561

— — Catalogue of the more valuable publications of the U. S. Government. Washington:
1885.   C 562

— — List of publications of the U. S. Government on the subject of Interoceanic Communi-
cation by the way of the American Isthmus.
Washington: 1885.   C 563

BIBLIOGRAPHY of the U. S. National Museum,
1882-3, [in Ann. Reports of the Smithsonian
Institution for 1882-3]. Washington: 1883-4.
        B 564

CATALOGUE. See No. 302.

FORD, P. L. A list of Treasury Reports and
Circulars issued by Alexander Hamilton, 1789-
1795. Brooklyn: 1886.   B 565 ‡

HICKOX, J. H. Monthly Catalogue U. S. publications. Nos. I to —. Washington: 1885 —
        B 566

LETTER from the Secretary of the Interior, trans-
mitting a list of books, etc., printed by this
Department from 1789 to 1881. Washington:
1882.   B 567
    47th Cong., 1st Sess. Senate Ex. Doc. No. 182.

LIST of Congressional documents from the 20th
to the 46th Congress. Washington: 1882.
        B 568 ‡

LIST of documents and other publications of the
U. S. from October, 1880, to April, 1881. [New
York: 1881.]   B 569

LIST of publications of the Engineer Department. Washington: 1876.   B 570

LIST of publications of the Engineers' Department U. S. Army, sent to the Inter. Cong. of
Geog. Science at Paris. Washington: 1875.
        B 571

LIST of Reports. See No. 340.

LIST of Reports, Maps, etc., forwarded by the
Engineers' Bureau of the War Dep. to the Inter. Geog. Cong. at Vienna. Washington:
1881.   B 572

PATTERSON, C. P. See No. 216.

POORE, B. P. Descriptive Catalogue of the
Government Publications of the U. S., 1774-
1881. Washington: 1885.   R 573 ‡

RHEE, W. J. Catalogue of Publications of the
Smithsonian Inst. Washington: 1882.
        B 573 (2) ‡ * †

SIMMONS, G. Catalogue of Books, embracing
Colonial and State publications and U. S.
Government publications. Washington: 1878.
        C 574

U. S. Government Publications, 1881-1884, [in
American Catalogue, 1876-84]. New York:
1885. See also No. 553.   B 557

Imprints.

DUBBS, J. H. Early Publications. Literary Ac-
tivity as Developed at Ephrata, [in Lancaster
Farmer, May, 1880].   576
    Also in "The Lancaster Examiner and Express,"
July 16, 1881.

HILDEBURN, C. R. The Issues of the Press in
Pennsylvania, 1685–1784. Philadelphia: 1885.
B 577 ‡ *
— — List of the Publications issued in Pennsyl-
vania, 1685 to [1776]. Philadelphia: 1882.
B 578 ‡
— — List of the issues of the Press in Pennsyl-
vania, [in Bull. Lib. Co. of Philadelphia].
Philadelphia: 1884–5. B 579 ‡
LEE, J. M W. *See* No. 723.
MUNSELL, J. Bibliotheca Munselliana, 1828–
1870. Albany: 1872. B 580 ‡ *
PUBLICATIONS of Christopher Sower. [Philadel-
phia: 1876.] B 581 ‡
SEIDENSTICKER. *See* No. 253.
STICKNEY, J. A. Anti-Revolutionary Publica-
tions in New Hampshire, [in Granite Month.,
V, p. 390]. Concord: 1882. B 582 ‡
SWIFT, L. Books printed by Benjamin Frank-
lin, [in Cat. of works relating to]. Boston:
1883. B 583 |
   Also in Boston Pub. Lib. Bull.
WESTCOTT, T. American books advertised in
the Pa. Gazette, 1728–1765, [in Hist. Mag., IV,
pp. 73, 235, and 328]. New York: 1861.
B 584 ‡
ZAHM, S. H. Catalogue of Rare Americana,
Principally Early Pennsylvanian Imprints.
Lancaster, Penn., No. 2, Sept., 1883. C 585

Periodicals.
Classed under
   Newspapers and Magazines.
   Almanacs.

Newspapers and Magazines.
ALDEN, E. American Annual Catalogue of
Newspapers. Cincinnati: 1878. 586
   A new edition issued each year.
AYERS & Sons' Manual, containing a catalogue of
all newspapers and periodicals published in the
U. S. and Canada. Philadelphia: 1883. 587
BOSS, H. R. Early newspapers in Illinois. Chi-
cago: 1870. 588
COGGESHALL, W. T. The Newspaper Record,
containing a complete list of newspapers and
periodicals. Philadelphia: 1856. 589
CURTISS, D. S. Newspapers of Wisconsin, Illi-
nois, and Iowa, [in Western Portraiture, p. 343].
New York: 1852. 590
FOLLETT, F. History of the Press in Western
New York. Rochester: 1847. 591
FREEZE, J. G. List of newspapers published in
Columbia Co., Pa., [in History of Columbia
Co., p. 187]. 1883. 592
GERHARD, F. List of Illinois newspapers, [in
Ill. as it is, p. 438]. Chicago: 1857. 593
GODDARD, D. O: Newspapers in New England,
1787–1815. Boston: 1880. 594
HUBBARD, H. P. Right Hand Record and news-
paper directory. New Haven: 1880. 595
HUTCHINSON, C. C. List of newspapers, [in
Resources of Kansas, p. 168]. Topeka: 1871.
596
KANSAS Newspapers and Periodicals. List of, [in

Fourth Bienn. Rep. of Kan. State Hist. Soc.].
1885. L 597

KENNY, D. J. American Newspaper Directory.
New York: 1861. 598

KING, W. L. The newspaper press of Charleston.
Charleston: 1870. 599

LEE, J. W. M. List of Newspapers in the Maryland Hist. Soc. Library. [in Mag. of Am. Hist.,
VI, p. 468] New York: 1881. 599 (1)

LIST of American newspapers and periodicals, [in
Bull. Boston Pub. Lib.]. Boston: 1879. 600

LIST of first newspapers in each state, [in Bookmart, I, p. 134]. Pittsburg: 1882. 601

LUERSTEDT, B. Swedish Newspapers and Periodicals published in the U. S., [in Report of the
Swedish Royal Library for 1885]. Stockholm:
1886. 602

McFARLAND, A. Early newspapers published in
Concord, N. H., [in Granite Monthly, II, p.
165]. Concord: 1879. 603

MATHEWS, J. B., and others. The Comic Periodical Literature of the U. S., [in the American
Bibliopolist, VII, pp. 199 and 264]. New York:
1875. 604

MEIKLE, W. The Canadian Newspaper Directory.
Toronto: 1858. 605

NEWSPAPERS in the Am. Antiq. Soc. Library,
[in Cat. of the Library]. Worcester: 1837.
L 606 *

NORTH, S. N. D. The Newspaper and Periodi-
cal Press of the U. S. Washington: 1884.
B 607
Also in U. S. Census, VIII.

PACKARD, J. List of newspapers, [in History of
La Porte Co., Ind., p. 459]. La Porte: 1876.
608

PETTENGILL, S. M. Advertisers' Handbook, a
list of newspapers, periodicals, and magazines.
New York: 1870. 609
A new edition issued each year.

POOLE, W. F. List of American Periodicals, [in
Index, I, p. xiv]. 610

ROWELL, G. P. American Newspaper Directory.
New York: 1871. 611
A new edition issued each year.

— — American Newspaper Directory, 1776. New
York: 1876. 612

— — Centennial Newspaper Exhibition, 1876.
New York: 1876. 613

STEIGER, E. The Periodical Literature of the
United States. New York: 1873. 614

STEVENS, Henry. American Books with tails to
'em. London: 1873. R 615 *

STREETER, S. L. Account of Newspapers and
other Periodicals published in Salem, from 1768
to 1856. Salem: 1886. 616

THOMAS, G. List of newspapers published in the
U. S. in 1775, [in History of Printing, II, p.
515]. 617

— — List of papers published in the U. S. in
1810, [in History of Printing, II, 517]. Worcester: 1810. 618

WHEELER, J. H. Press of North Carolina, [in
Historical Sketches of N. C., p. 112]. Philadelphia: 1851. 619

Almanacs.

FITTS, J. H. The Thomas Almanacs. [Salem: 1886.] 620
Also in Essex Inst. Hist. Coll., XII

PERRY, Amos. Some New England Almanacs. Providence: 1885. 621

STICKNEY, M. A. Almanacs and their Authors, [in Hist. Coll. Essex Inst., VIII and XIV]. Salem: 1878. 622

Poetry.

DUBBS, J. H. Early German Hymnology of Pennsylvania [1882]. 623
Also in Ref. Quarterly Review, Oct., 1888.

HARRIS, C. F. Index to American Poetry and Plays. Providence: 1874. R 624 *

KETTELL, S. Chronological Catalogue of American Poetry, [in Specimens of Am. Poetry, III, 379]. Boston: 1829. B 625 ‡

ROWELL, J. C. List of Works containing American Sonnets, [in Sonnet in America, p. 19], by J. C. Rowell. Oakland: 1887. 626

STOCKBRIDGE, J. C. A Catalogue of the Harris Collection of American Poetry. Providence: 1886. L 627 *

Miscellaneous.

LIST of American Books on Sports and Outdoo Amusements, [in Trade Circular, June]. New York: 1870. 628

LIST of American writers upon Biblical archæology and exploration in Bible lands, [in Old Testament Student, June, p. 303]. 629

LIST of publications by members of certain college faculties and learned societies in the U. S., 1867–1872, [Circulars of information, No. 4, U. S. Bureau of Education]. Washington: 1873. 630

LITERATURE of American Journalism, [in Boston Pub. Lib. Bull., II, p. 427]. 631

REFERENCE Notes on American Journalism, [in Lib. Bull. of Cornell Univ., I, p. 329]. Ithaca: 1885. R 632

SOLBERG, G. Bibliography of literary property, [in Bowker's Copyright, its laws and literature]. New York: 1886. B 633

TIFFANY, J. K. A Catalogue of Stamp Publications. St. Louis: 1874. 634

TRUMBULL, J. H. The New England Primer and its Predecessors, [in The Sunday-School Times, April 29 and May 6]. 1882. 635

— — Catechisms of Old and New England, [in The Sunday-School Times, Sept. 3 and 15]. 1883. 636

LOCAL DIVISIONS.

Classed under
  General Works.
  New England.
  Middle States.
  Southern States.
  Mississippi Valley.
  Rocky Mountains and Pacific Coast

General Works.

DURRIE, D. S. List of Local Histories, [in Index to Am. Pedigrees.] Albany: 1887. B 637
  Earlier editions, 1868 and 1878.

[GRIFFIN, A. P. C.] Index of Articles upon American Local History in periodicals, transactions, and collections, [in Bost. Pub. Lib. Bull., V, 330, and still publishing]. B 638 †

LUDEWIG, H. E. Literature of American Local History. New York: 1846. B 639 †

MEMORANDA of Local Histories in the Library of the Am. Antiq. Society. Worcester: 1869. R 640 †

PERKINS, F. B. Check list for American Local History. Boston: 1876. R 641 †
  Also in Boston Pub. Lib. Bull.

WOODWARD, C. L. American Topographs. Catalogues Nos. 10, 15, 18, 22, 27, and 31. New York: 1877-1888. B 642 †

New England.

AUTHORITIES on Norumbege, [in Bull. Boston Pub. Lib., III, p. 271]. 643

COOLIDGE, A. J., and Mansfield, J. B. Historical Works on New England, [in a Hist. and Description of N. E., I, p. xi]. Boston: 1859. B 644

DEANE, C. Sources of information relative to New England, [in No. 143, III, p. 340]. R 645

DE COSTA, B. F. Sources of information relative to Norumbega, [in No. 143, III, p. 169]. R 646

GODDARD, D. O. See No. 594.

HAYWARD. See No. 205.

LITTLEFIELD, G. Catalogue of New England Histories, [Nos. 2, 3, and 4]. Boston: 1881. C 647

PALFREY, J. G. See No. 214.

PERRY, A. See No. 621.

REFERENCE list on Social Life in New England, [in Monthly Reference List, III, pp. 26 and 31]. R 648

WINSOR, J. See No. 224.

— — Sources of information relative to New England, [in No. 143, p. 156]. R 649

Maine.

AUTHORITIES on the Popham Colony, [in Boston Pub. Lib. Bull., III, p. 272]. R 650

COOLIDGE, A. J., and Mansfield, J. B. List of Works on Maine, [in a History of New England, I, p. xvi]. Boston: 1859. B 651

GRIFFIN, J. Bibliography of Books printed in and written by Maine Authors, [in History of the Press in Me., p. 215]. 1872. B 652

POOLE, W. F., and Ballard, E. Bibliography of the Popham Colony, [in The Popham Colony, p. 65]. Boston: 1866. B 653

WARDEN, D. B. Works relating to the History of Maine, [in Account of the U. S., p. 370]. Edinburgh: 1819. B 654 ‡

WILLIS, W. Bibliography of Maine. New York: 1859. B 655 *

Also in Norton's Lit. Letter, No. 4.

— — Descriptive Catalogue of Books relating to Maine, [in Hist. Mag., XVII, p. 145]. New York: 1865. B 656*

New Hampshire.

CHASE, F. Bibliography of Dartmouth College, [in Granite Monthly, V, p. 321]. Concord: 1882. B 657

COOLIDGE, A. J., and Mansfield, J. B. List of Works on New Hampshire, [in History of New England, p. xx]. Boston: 1859. B 658

COTTON, A. E. New Hampshire Authors, [in Granite Month., X, p. 214]. Concord: 1887. B 659

EASTMAN, S. C. Catalogue of Books relating to New Hampshire, [in Norton's Literary Letter, new series, No. 1]. New York: 1859. B 660 *

LIST of Election Sermons before the N. H. Legislature, [in Allen's Election Sermon, 1818]. Concord: 1818. R 661

LIST of New Hampshire Town Histories, [in Granite Month., II, p. 285]. Concord : 1879. B 662

McCLINTOCK. Bibliography of New Hampshire, [in Granite Month., IV, p. 286]. Concord: 1881. B 663

McFARLAND, A. *See* No. 603.

MOORE, J. W. Bibliography of Manchester, N. H. Manchester: 1885. B 664 *

STEVENS, H. A Catalogue of Books and Pamphlets relating to New Hampshire. London: 1885. C 665 *

STICKNEY, J. A. *See* No. 582.

WARDEN, D. B. Works relating to the History of New Hampshire, [in Account of the U. S., I, p. 417]. Edinburgh: 1819. B 666 ‡

Vermont.

COOLIDGE, A. J., and Mansfield, J. B. List of Works on Vermont, [in History of N. E., I, p. xxiv]. Boston: 1859. B 667

GILMAN, M. D. Bibliography of Vermont, [in Argus and Patriot, Jan. 29, 1879, to Sept. 22, 1880]. Montpelier: 1879–80.   B 668

HALL, B. Bibliography of Vermont, [New York: 1860].   B 669 *
Also in Norton's Literary Letter, new series, No. 2.

LIST of Election Sermons of Vermont, [in Historical Mag.].   R 670 ‡

LIST of pamphlets published by the Vermont Hist. Soc., [in Coll. of, II, p. v]. Montpelier: 1871.   B 671 ‡

Massachusetts.

ANCIENT and Honorable Artillery Co. List of Sermons preached before the, 1659–1882, [244 Ann. Record of]. Boston: 1882.   R 672 ‡
Earlier lists in Lathrop's Sermon, 1838, and Rules and Reg., 1863.

BOSTON. *See* No. 477.

CHASE, H. E. *See* No. 255.

COLBURN, J. Bibliography of Local History of Mass. Boston: 1871.   B 673 †

DEXTER, F. B. Sources of information relative to Plymouth Colony, [in No. 143, III, p. 283].   R 674

EDES, H. E. List. of Mass. Election Sermons, [in Sermon for 1871]. Boston: 1871. R 675 ‡
Earlier lists in Sermons for 1794, 1809, 1836, 1849, and 1866.

ESSEX Institute. Priced Catalogue of the Publications of the. Salem: 1881.   B 676 ‡

FOSTER, W. E. Reference list on the Foundling of Boston, [in Lib. Jour., Sept.–Oct.]. New York: 1880.   R 677

GREEN, S. A. Bibliography of the Massachusetts Hist. Society. Boston: 1871.   B 678 ‡

HARVARD University. List of Publications of, and its officers, 1870–1880. Cambridge: 1882.   B 679 *
— 1880–85. Cambridge: 1886.   B 679 (2) *

HUMANE Society. List of Discourses delivered before the, [in History of the Humane Soc. of Mass., p. 32]. Boston: 1845.   R 680 ‡

HUNNEWELL, J F. Bibliography of Charlestown and Bunker Hill. Boston : 1881.   B 681

LEXINGTON, Concord, and Bunker's Hill. *See* No. 474.

NICHOLS, W. R. Publications of the Mass. Institute of Technology, and its officers, students, and alumni, 1861–1881. Boston: 1882. B 682

PAINE, N. Publications of the American Antiquarian Soc. Worcester: 1883.   B 683 †

PORTER, E. List of Sermons before the Annual Convention of Congregational Ministers of Mass., [in Sermon delivered before]. Boston: 1810.   R 684 †

SHURTLEFF, N. B. Maps and Plans of Boston, [in A Topographical and Hist. Description of Boston, p. 91]. Boston: 1871.   685

SIBLEY, J. L. Notices of the Triennial and Annual Catalogues of Harvard University. Boston: 1865.   686

SMITH, N. B. Maps of Boston, [in Proc. of the Mass. Hist. Soc., 1862–3, p. 37]. Boston: 1863.   687

SPOFFORD, J. List of books on Massachusetts, [in Gaz. of, p. 6]. Newburyport: 1828. 688

STREETER, G. L. *See* No. 616.

WARDEN, D. B. Books relating to Massachusetts, [in Account of the U. S., I, p. 346]. Edinburgh: 1819]. B 689 †

WEBSTER, D. List of Discourses delivered at Plymouth, in commemoration of, Dec. 22, 1620, [in "Discourse," p. 103]. Boston: 1821. R 690 †

WILLIAMS College. Publications of the President and Professors of, 1793–1876. North Adams: 1876. 691

WORCESTER, Bibliography of, [in Celebration of the 200th Anniversary of the Naming, p. 167]. Worcester: 1885. B 692

YOUNG, A. List of Dudleian Lectures, 1755–1846, [in Young's Discourse]. Boston: 1846. R 693 †

Rhode Island.

BARTLETT, J. R. Bibliography of Rhode Island. Providence: 1864. B 694 *

HAMMETT, C. E. Bibliography of Newport, R. I. Newport: 1887. B 695 * †

WARDEN, D. B. Books relating to Rhode Island, [in Account of the U. S., I, p. 479]. Edinburgh: 1819. B 696 †

Connecticut.

GILMAN, D. C. Books on Connecticut, [in Contrib. to the Ecclesiastical History of, p. 560]. New Haven: 1861. B 697

JOHNSTON, A. Bibliography, [in American Commonwealths, Connecticut, p. 397]. Boston: 1887. R 698

LEE, C. List of Connecticut Election Sermons, [in Sermon for 1813]. Hartford: 1813. R 699 *

Middle States.

ASHER, G. M. *See* Nos. 47 and 195.

BIBLIOGRAPHIA Sueco. *See* No. 279.

FERNOW, B. Sources of information relative to the Middle Colonies, [in No. 143, V, p. 231]. R 700

— — Sources of information relative to New Netherlands, [in No. 143, IV, p. 409]. R 701

KEEN, G. B. Sources of information relative to New Sweden, [in No. 143, IV, p. 488]. R 702

New York.

CORNELL University. Recent publications by officers of, [in Cornell Library, I, pp. 245, 261, and 281]. Ithaca: 1884-5. 703

DAWSON, H. B. Maps of the large estates on which the city of New York now stands, [in Hist. Mag., XXII, p. 206]. Morrisania: 1873. 704

EAST River Bridge, [in Monthly Ref. List, III, p. 22]. R 705

FOLLETT, F. *See* No. 591.

LONG ISLAND. Bibliography of, [in American Bibliopolist, IV, 539]. New York: 1872. B 706 †

MUNSELL, J. *See* No. 580.

— F. Bibliography of Albany. Albany: 1885. B 707 †

NEW YORK Historical Society, Publications of, [covers of " Proceedings " of the Soc. for 1848]. New York: 1848. B 708 †

ONDERDONK, H. Bibliography of Long Island, [in Antiquities of, by G. Furman, p. 435]. New York: 1875. B 709 *

REFERENCE list of Authorities on History and Settlement of Western New York, [in Cornell Library, I, p. 181]. Ithaca: 1883. R 710

STEVENS, J. A. Sources of information relative to New York, [in No. 143, III, p. 411]. R 711

WARDEN, D. B. Books relating to New York, [in Account of the U. S., I, p. 551]. Edinburgh: 1819. B 712 †

New Jersey.

[VINTON, F.] Catalogue of Books written by the Alumni and Officers of the College of New Jersey. Philadelphia: 1876. 713

WHITEHEAD, W. A. Sources of information relative to East and West Jersey, [in No. 143, III, p. 449]. R 714

— — Catalogue of Books on New Jersey during the Colonial Period, [in Analytical Index to the Colonial Docs., p. 477. Newark: 1858. B 715 †

Pennsylvania.

DUBBS, J. H. See Nos. 576 and 623.

FREEZE, J. G. See No. 592.

HAYDEN, H. E. A Bibliography of the Wyoming Valley, [in Proc. and Coll. of the Wyoming Hist. and Geol. Soc., III, p. 68]. Wilkesbarre: 1885. B 716

HILDEBURNE, C. R. See Nos. 577–9.

LESLIE, J. P. See No. 338.

PHILADELPHIA, [in Monthly Ref. List, II, p. 39]. R 716 (2)

PITTSBURG, Bibliography of, [in Bookmart, II, 328, 329]. Pittsburg: 1882. B 717

PUBLICATIONS of Sower. See No. 581.

SEIDENSTICKER. See No. 253.

STONE, F. D. Bi-centennial Reading on the founding of Philadelphia, [in Bull. Lib. Co. of Phila., p. 65]. Philadelphia: R 718

— — Sources of information relative to Pennsylvania, [in No. 143, III, p. 495]. R 719

SWIFT, L. See No. 583.

WARDEN, D. B. List of Books on Pennsylvania, [in Account of the U. S., II, 119]. -Edinburgh: 1819. B 720 †

WESTCOTT, T. See No. 584.

ZAHN, S. H. See No. 585.

Maryland.

BRANTLY, W. T. Sources of information relative to Maryland, [in No. 143, III, p. 553]. R 721

JOHNS Hopkins University. Bibliographia Hopkinsiensis, 1876–1882, [in 7th Ann. Rep. of the President]. Baltimore: 1882. B 722

LEE, J. M. W. A hand list of Laws, Journals, and Documents of Maryland to 1800. Baltimore: 1878. B 723

— — Bibliography of the Baltimore and Ohio Railroad. London: 1879. B 724

MORRIS, J. G. Bibliography of Maryland, [in Hist. Mag., XVII, pp. 240, 328]. New York: 1870.   B 725 *

PUBLICATIONS of the Maryland Historical Society, 1844-85, [in Annual Report for 1884-85]. Baltimore: 1885.   B 726

WARDEN, D. B. Books relating to Maryland, [in Account of the U. S., II, p. 165]. Edinburgh: 1819.   B 727 †

WINSOR, J. Sources of information relative to Maryland and Virginia, [in No. 143, V, p. 270].
                                                      R 728

Southern States.

Virginia.

ADAMS, H. B. A Bibliography of William and Mary College, [in Circulars of Information of the Bureau of Education, No. 1]. Washington: 1887.   B 729 *

BROCK, R. A. Sources of information relative to Virginia, [in No. 143, III, p. 153].   R 730

COOKE, J. E. List of Authorities on Virginia, [in Am. Commonwealths, Virginia, p. i]. Boston: 1883.   B 731

JONES, J. W. *See* No. 167.

WARDEN, D. B. Works on Virginia, [in Account of the U. S., II, p. 227]. Edinburgh: 1819.   B 732 †

WINSOR, J. *See* No. 230.

—— and others. Authorities on the early history of Virginia, [in Bull. Boston Public Lib., III, p. 269]. Boston: 1877.   R 733

YORKTOWN. *See* Nos. 480 and 486.

The Carolinas.

KING, W. L. *See* No. 599.

WARDEN, D. B. Works on North and South Carolina, [in Account of the U. S., pp. 393 and 455]. Edinburgh: 1819.   B 734 †

WHEELER, J. H. *See* No. 619.

WINSOR, J. Sources of information relative to the Carolinas, [in No. 143, V, p. 285].   R 735

Georgia.

BIBLIOGRAPHY of Georgia, [in Literary World, XIV, p. 241]. 1883.   B 736

GEORGIA, [in Monthly Ref. List, III, p. 10].
                                                      B 737

JONES, C. C., Jr. Sources of information relative to Georgia, [in No. 143, V, p. 392].   738

SHEA, J. G. *See* No. 743.

WARDEN, D. B. Books relating to Georgia, [in Account of the U. S., II, p. 488]. Edinburgh: 1819.   B 739 †

Florida.

BOIMARE, A. L. Notes Bibliographiques et raisonées sur les principaux ouvrage publiés sur la Floride et l'ancienne Louisiane. Paris: 1855.   740

BRINTON, D. G. Literary history of Florida, [in Notes on the Floridian peninsula, p. 13]. Philadelphia: 1859.   741

GAFFAREL, P. Notice bibliographique sur Florida, [in Histoire de la Floride, p. 337]. Paris: 1875.   742

SHEA, J. G. Sources of information relative to Ancient Florida, [in No. II, p. 299].   R 743

Mississippi Valley.
General Works.

BALDWIN, C. C. *See* No. 196.

BARTLETT, J. R. *See* No. 459.

CATALOGUE. *See* No. 302.

COUES, E. *See* No. 373.

CURTIS, D. S. *See* No. 590.

DUNN, J. P. *See* No. 256.

GRIFFIN, A. P. C. *See* No. 164.

HOWE, H. Authorities on Western History, [in Hist. Collections of the Great West, p. 30]. Cincinnati: 1851.   B 744

KNIGHT, G. W. Books on the North West Territory, [in Papers of the Am. Hist. Assoc., I, p. 173]. New York: 1886.   R 745

NEILL, E. *See* No. 174.

NORTHWEST, [in Monthly Reference List, III, p. 41].   R 746

PARKMAN, F. *See* No. 215.

PECK, J. M. Historical References for the Valley of the Mississippi, [in the American Pioneer, II, 262, 314]. Cincinnati: 1843.   B 747

PERKINS, J. H. Authorities, [in Annals of the West, p. xviii]. Cincinnati: 1846.   748

SHINN, C. H. *See* No. 392.

WARREN, G. K. List of Works on the Exploration of the West, [in Reports of Explorations and Surveys for a railroad from the Mississippi to the Pacific, XI, 17]. Washington: 1855   B 749 †

Alabama.

WARDEN, D. B. Books relating to Alabama, [in Account of the U. S., III, p. 41]. Edinburgh: 1819.   B 750 †

Dakota.

WILLIAMS, J. F. Bibliography of Dakota, [in Coll. of the Minnesota Hist. Soc., III, p. 37]. St. Paul: 1870.   B 751 †

Illinois.

BOSS, H. R. *See* No. 588.

GERHARD, F. *See* No. 593.

Indiana.

PACKARD, J. *See* No. 608.

YOHN, A. B. Catalogue of Books relating to Indiana. Indianapolis: 1877.   C 752

Kansas.

HOLLOWAY, J. N. Works relating to Kansas, [in History of Kansas, p. 580]. Lafayette: 1868.   B 753

HUTCHINSON, C. C. *See* No. 596.

KANSAS Newspapers. *See* No. 597.

SPRING, L. W. Bibliography of Kansas, [in Am. Commonwealths, Kansas, p. 323]. Boston: 1885.   B 754

Kentucky.

DURRETT, R. T. List of books relating to Kentucky, [in Am. Commonwealths, Kentucky, by N. S. Shaler]. Boston: 1885.   B 755

Louisiana.

FARIBAULT. *See* No. 73.

NEW ORLEANS and Louisiana, [in Monthly Reference List, IV, p. 34].   R 756

THOMASSY. *See* No. 219.

WARDEN, D. B. Books relating to Louisiana, [in Account of the U. S., II, p. 568]. Edinburgh: 1819.   B 757 †

WINSOR, J. *See* No. 223.

Minnesota.

WILLIAMS, J. F. Bibliography of Minnesota. St. Paul: 1870.   B 758

    Also in Minn. Hist. Soc. Coll., III, p. 13.

Missouri.

SWALLOW, G. C. *See* No. 350.

WARDEN, D. B. Works relating to Missouri, [in Account of the U. S., III, p. 158]. Edinburgh: 1819.   B 759 †

Ohio.

THOMAS, C. Bibliography of the Earthworks of Ohio, [in Ohio Arch. and Historical Quarterly, I, 69, 191, 272]. Cincinnati: 1887.   B 760

— — early books which treat of the Earthworks of Ohio, [in Am. Antiquarian and Oriental Journ., IX, 239]. Cincinnati: 1887.   B 761

THOMSON, P. G. Bibliography of Ohio. Cincinnati: 1880.   B 762 * ‡

WARDEN, D. B. Books relating to Ohio, [in Account of the U. S., II, p. 279]. Edinburgh: 1819.   B 763 †

Texas.

ANDERSON, A. D. Works on Texas, [in The Silver Country, p. 157]. New York: 1877.   B 764 *

OLMSTEAD, F. L. List of works on Texas, [in A Journey through Texas, p. 495]. New York: 1857.   B 765

Wisconsin.

DURRIE, D. C. Bibliography of Wisconsin, [in Hist. Mag.]. New York: 1870.   B 766 *

LIST of books relating to Wisconsin, [in Catalogue of the library of the State Historical Soc. of Wisconsin, I, p. 559]. Madison: 1873.   L 767

    Also Supplement, p. 373.
    Also Vol. IV, p. 731.

Rocky Mountains and Pacific Coast.

General Works.

ANDERSON, A. D. Works on the West, [in The Silver Country, p. 168]. New York: 1877.   B 768 *

BANCROFT, H. H. *See* No. 254.

BANCROFT, H. H. Works on the Northwest Coast, [in Hist. of the Pacific States, XXII, p. 26]. San Francisco: 1884.   B 769 *

BEAN, T. H. *See* No. 318.

DUFLOT DE MOFRAS, M. Authorities on the Pacific Coast, [in Exploration du territoire de l'Oregon, des Californies, etc.]. Paris: 1844.   770

GILL, T. *See* No. 319–20.

Alaska.

BANCROFT, H. H. Works on Alaska, [in Hist. of the Pacific States, XXVIII, p. 23]. San Francisco: 1886. B 771 *

DALL, W. H., and Baker, M. Partial List of books, pamphlets, papers in serial, journals, etc., on Alaska, [in U. S. Coast and Geodectic Survey, Pacific Coast Pilot, p. 225]. Washington: 1879. B 772

DALL, William H. List of works containing information in regard to Alaska, [in Alaska and its resources]. Boston : 1870. B 773

GREWINGK, C. Authorities on Alaska, [in Beitrag zur Kenntniss der oragraphischen und geognostischen Beschaffenheit der Nord West Küste Amerikas, p. 294], by C. Grewingk. St. Petersburg : 1850. 774

MURDOCH, J. See No. 448.

SUMNER, C. Sources of Information upon Alaska, [in Works of, XI, p. 234]. Boston : 1877. 775

Arizona.

ANDERSON, A. D. Works on Arizona, [in The Silver Country, p. 164]. New York : 1877. B 776 *

California.

ANDERSON, A. D. Works on California, [in The Silver Country, p. 149]. New York : 1877. B 777 *

BANCROFT, H. H. Works on California, [in Hist. of the Pacific States, XIII, p. 25]. San Francisco : 1884. B 778 *

CRONISE, T. F. Works on California, [in The Natural Wealth of Cal., p. 694]. San Francisco : 1868. B 779 |

DIETZ, A. P. A list of books relating to California, [in Bibliotheca Californiæ. A Cat. of the State Library, II, p. 687]. Sacramento : 1874. L 780

LIST of publications by members of the teaching force of the University of California, [in Biennial report of the President of, p. 119]. San Francisco : 1886. B 781

MEMORIA de los autores que hablan de las Californias, [in Coleccion de documentos ineditos para la historia de España, by M. S. y D. P. G. de Baranda, XV, p. 225]. Madrid: 1849. 782

SCHLAGINTWEIT, R. Literature of California, [in Californien: Land und Leute, p. 369]. Coln: 1871. 783

TAYLOR, A. S. Bibliografa Californica: or notes and materials to aid in forming a bibliography of the Pacific Coast, [in Sacramento Daily Union, June 25]. Sacramento: 1863. B 784 *

Colorado.

ANDERSON, A. D. Works on Colorado, [in The Silver Country, p. 165]. New York: 1877. B 785 *

Nevada.

ANDERSON, A. D. Works on Nevada, [in The Silver Country, p. 166]. New York: 1877. B 786 *

New Mexico.

ANDERSON, A. D. Works on New Mexico, [in

The Silver Country, p. 163]. New York: 1877. B 787 *

HAYNES, H. W. Sources of information relative to the exploration of New Mexico, [in No. 143, II, p. 498]. R 788

Oregon.

BANCROFT, H. H. Works on Oregon, [in Hist. of the Pacific States, XXIV, p. 19]. San Francisco: 1886. B 789 *

BARROW, W. Works on Oregon, [in Am. Commonwealths, Oregon, p. i], Boston: 188–. 790

FOSTER, W. E. Bibliography of Oregon, [in Mag. of Am. Hist., VII, p. 461]. New York: 1881. R 790 (2)

Utah.

See also Theology—Mormons.

ANDERSON, A. D. Works on Utah, [in The Silver Country, p. 167]. New York: 1877. B 791 *

Wyoming.

PEALE, A. C. Bibliography, [in Report on Thermal Springs of the Yellowstone]. 792

POLITICAL DIVISIONS.

Mexico.

See also South America—General.

ANDERSON, A. D. American and English authorities on Mexico, [in Mexico from the material standpoint, p. 143]. New York: 1884. B 793 *

ANDRADE, J. M. Catalogue de la Rich Bibliothèque de. Leipzig: 1869. A 794 *

BANCROFT, H. H. Authorities on the Mexican States, [in Hist. of the Pacific States, X, p. 19]. San Francisco: 1879. B 795 *

— — Works on Mexico, [in Hist. of the Pacific States, XXI, iv]. San Francisco: 1883. B 795 (2) *

BANDELIER, A. F. See No. 823.

BARTLETT, J. R. List of books printed in Mexico, 1540–160–, [in No. 53, I, p. 131]. Providence: 1875. B 796 ‡

BERISTANI MARTIN DE SOUZA, J. M. Biblioteca Hispano-Americano Septentrional. Mexico: 1816. B 797

— — New edition. Amecameca: 1883.

BLISS, P. C. Bibliotheca Mexicana. New York: 1885. A 798 *

BOBAN. See No. 843.

BOOKS on the Conquest of Peru and Mexico. Cambridge: 1860. 799

BOTURINI BERNADUCE, L. List of books, maps, and mss. relating to the history and language of Mexico, [in Idea de una Historia General de la America Septentrional]. Madrid: 1746. 800

BRASSEUR DE BOURBOURG, M. Bibliothèque Mexico-Guatémalienne. Paris: 1871. B 801 *

CATALOGUE d'un livres relatifs a l'Amérique et particulièrement aux Mexico. Paris: 1857. A 802 *

CLAVIGERA, F. S. Notizia Degli Scuttori della Storia Autica del Messico, [in Storia Antica de Messico, p. 6]. Cesena: 1780. 803
Also in English edition of 1787.

EGUIARA y Eguren, J. J. de. Bibliotheca Mexicana. Mexico: 1755. B 804 *

FERRARIO, J. Works on Mexico, [in Le Costume, XVI, p. 508]. Milan: 1827. 805

[FISHER, Augustin.] Bibliotheca Mejicana. London: 1869. A 806 *

HARRISSE, H. See No. 79.

HELLER, C. B. List of books on Mexico, [in Reisen in Mexico, p. xv]. Leipzig: 1853. 807

ICAZBALCETA, J. G. See No. 288.

— — Bibliografia Mexicana del Siglo, XVI. Mexico: 1886. B 808 †

— — Books printed by A. C. Benavides in Mexico, [in Mem. de la Academia Mex., III, p. 44]. Mexico: 1886. B 809

— — La "Grandeza Mexicana," de Balbruna. Nota Bibliographica, [in Mem. de la Acad. Mex., III, p. 94]. Mexico: 1886. B 810

— — Bibliografia. Autores y ediciones, [in Mexico en 1554, p. 323]. Mexico: 1875. 812

MAYER, B. List of Authorities on Mexico, [in Mexico, Aztec, Spanish, and Republican, I, p. 3]. Hartford: 1853. 813

MEXICO, [in Monthly Ref. List, IV, p. 4]. R 814

NIOX, M. Maps of Mexico, [in Notice sur la Carte du Mexique, p. 19]. Paris: 1874. 815
Also in Bul. de la Soc. de Geographie, VI, series viii, 1874.

PINEDA. See No. 875.

RAMIREZ, J. F. Bibliotheca Mexicana. London: 1880. A 816 *

ROMERO, J. G. Noticia de las personas que han escritos o publicado algunas obras sobre idiomas que se hablan en la Republica, [in Bol. Soc. Mex. de Geog., VIII, p. 374]. Mexico: 1862. 817

SABIN, J. See No. 829 (2).

SAINT MARTIN, V. de. Books on Mexico, [in Rapport fait à la Commission scientifique du Mexico, p. 19]. Paris: 1865. 818

[TROSS, E.] Bibliotheca Mexicana. Paris: 1868. A 819 *

TRÜBNER, N. No. 10. Catalogue of Spanish books relating to Mexico. London: 1876. C 820

WINSOR, J. Sources of information relative to Mexican History, [in No. 143, II, p. 297]. R 821

Central America.

BANCROFT, H. H. Works on Central America, [in Hist. of the Pacific States, XXV]. San Francisco: 1882. B 822 *

BANDELIER, A. F. Notes on a Bibliography of Yucatan and Central America. Worcester: 1881. B 823

BOBAN. See No. 843.

BRASSEUR DE BOURBOURG. See No. 801.

DROUILLET, L. Bibliography of interoceanic

canals in Central America, [in Les Isthmes Américains, p. 310]. Paris: 1876. 824
Also in *L'Explorateur* of March 30, 1876.

LEVY, P. Bibliography and Cartography of Nicaraguanse. [in Notas Geograficas y Economicas, p. 597]. Paris: 1863. 825

NOURSE, J. E. Authorities on interoceanic canals in Central America, [in Report on Interoceanic Canals, p. 32], by C. H. Davis. Washington: 1867. ▪ 826

—— Authorities on the Nicaragua Canal, [in 43d Cong., 1st Sess., Ex. Doc., No. 57, p. 142]. Washington: 1874. 827

PIM, B., and Seaman, B. Bibliography of Central America, [in Dottings on the Roadside in Panama, Nicaragua, and Mosquito]. London: 1869. B 828

REICHARDT, C. F. Literatur über Centro-Amerika, [in Centro-Amerika, p. 255]. Braunschweig: 1851. 829

SABIN, J. Catalogue of the library of E. G. Squier. New York: 1876. A 829 (2) *

SCHERZER, C. Bibliography of Works on Central America, [in Wanderungen durch die Mittel - Americanischen, p. 510]. Braunschweig: 1857. 830

SIVERS, J. Von. Works on the Antilles, Central America, and New Spain, [in Ueber Madeira und die Antillen, p. 311]. Leipzig: 1861. B 831

SQUIER, E. G. Bibliography of Central America, [in The States of Central America, p. 766]. New York: 1858. B 832

—— Bibliography of Central America, [in Notes on Central America, p. 389]. New York: 1855. B 833

Bermuda.

LEFROY, J. H. Bibliography of the Bermudas, [in Memorial of Bermuda, II, p. xi]. London: 1886. B 834

West Indies.

BACHILLER y Morales, A. Catalogue of publications in Cuba from 1724 to 1840, [in Apuntes para la Historia de las Letras, etc. ... de la Cuba]. Habana: 1859–1861. B 835

BONNEAU, A. Haïti, ses progrès—et une Bibliographie d'Haïti. Paris: E. Dentu, 1862. 836

EDEN, C. Bibliography [in The West Indies]. London : 1881. B 837 *

HAZARD, S. List of Works on Cuba, [in Cuba with Pen and Pencil, p. v.]. Hartford : 1871. 838

—— Bibliography of Santo Domingo and Hayti, [in Santo-Domingo, past and present, p. xxi], by Samuel Hazard]. New York ! 1873. B 839

SAINT-REMY, R. L. de. Bibliography of Saint-Domingo, [in Saint-Domingo, II, 572]. Paris: 1846. 840

SIVERS, J. von. Works on Cuba, [in Cuba, die Perle der Antillen, p. 341]. Leipzig: 1861. 841

[WURDIMAN, F.]. Works relating to Cuba, [in Notes on Cuba, p. v.], by a Physician. Boston: 1844. 842

South America.

See also America, general works.

General Works.

BODAN collection of Antiquities. Books.—
Manuscript and Printed. New York: 1880.
A 843 *

GUTIERREZ, J. M. Estudios sobre algunos poetas sud Americanos. Buenos Aires: 1865. 844

LONG, G. and others. Works on South America, [in America and the West Indies, p. 631]. London: 1845. 845

MAFFEI, E. *See* No. 341.

MANTEGAZZA, P. Bibliography of South America, [in Sulla America Meridionale, p. 344]. Milano: 1858. 846

MULHALL, M. G. and E. T. Works on the River Plate, [in Handbook of the River Plate Republics, (Buenos Aires, Argentine Confederation, Uruguay and Paraguay) p. 407]. London: 1875. 847

SOLDANHA da Gama, J. de. Works on South America, [in Catalogo de Exposicao de Bibliotheca Nacional. Rio de Janeira: 1885. 848

TRÜBNER, N. Bibliotheca Hispano-Americano. London: 1870. 848 (2)

— — New edition. London: 1878. 848 (3)

Argentine Republic.

ANDREE, K. Works on the Argentine Republic, [in Buenos Aires und die Argentinischen Provinzen, p. xiv], by Karl Andree. Leipzig: 1856. 849

GUTIERREZ, J. M. Apuntes biograficos de escritu.,es, ovades y hombres de Bepublica Argentina. Buenos Aires: 1860. 850

— — Bibliografia de la primera imprenta de Buenos Aires. Buenos Aires. 1866. B 851 (1)

INFORME sobre la collection de obras Argentinas, [in Biblioteca Pub. de Buenos Aires]. Buenos Aires: 1878. 851 (2)

MULHALL. *See* No. 847.

MOUSSY, V. M. de. List of Authorities on the Agentine Confederation, [in Description géographique et statistique de la Confederation Argentine, IV, p. 3]. Paris: 1864. 852

TRÜBNER, N. Works on the Argentine Republic, [in Literary Guide, Nos. 9, 14, and 16]. London: 1865-6. B 853 †

Bolivia.

BALLIVIAN y Roxas, V. de. Catalogue of books on Bolivia, [in Archivo Boliviano, I, 507]. Paris: 1872. 854

CORTES, J. D. Bibliography of Bolivia, [in Bolivia apuntes geográficos, etc., p. 155]. Paris: 1875. 855

ORBIGNY, A. d'. List of maps of Bolivia, [in Voyage dans l'Amerique Méredionale, p. 244]. Paris: 1846. 856

RENÉ-Moreno, S. Biblioteca Boliviano. Santiago de Chili: 1879. 857

Brazil.

ASHER, G. M. *See* No. 47.

AZEVEDO Marques, M. E. de. List of Authorities on Brazil, [in Apontamentos Historicos, etc., p. xiii]. Rio de Janeiro: 1879.   858

BARIL, V. L. Works on Brazil, [in L'Empire du Brézil, p. xiv]. Paris: 1862.   859

BLAKE, A. V. A. S. Diccionario Bibliographico Brazileiro. Rio de Janeiro: 1883.   860

BURTON, A. F. List of Works on Brazil, [in The Highlands of Brazil, p. 13]. London: 1869.   861

CABRAL, A. Work on Brazil, [in Revista do Inst. Hist. e Geog. de Brazil, III, p. 171]. Rio de Janeiro: 1852.   862

DENIS, F. Bibliography of the principal works on the region of the Amazon River, [in Esplorazione delle regione equatoriale, p. 321]. Milano: 1854.   863

FLETCHER, J. C., and Kidder, D. P. Works on Brazil, [in Brazil and the Brazilians, p. vi]. Boston: 1866.   864

GALVÂS, B. F. R. and Saldanha da Gama, J. Catalogo da Esposiçâo de Historia do Brazil. Rio de Janeiro: 1881-3.   865

HANDELMANN, H. Literature of Brazil, [in Geschichte von Brazilien, p. 968]. Berlin: 1860.   866

LIMA, A. H. de. Works on Brazil, [in Catalogo da Bibliotheca Municipal de Rio de Janeiro]. Rio de Janeiro: 1878.   867

MARKHAM, C. R. List of Authorities on the Valley of the Amazon, [in Expedition into the Valley of the Amazons, p. 146]. London: 1859.   868

MONTENEY, B. Works on Brazil, [in Selections from the Authors who have written concerning Brazil, p. 180]. London: 1825.   869

MULHALL, M. G. and E. T. Works on Brazil, [in Handbook of Brazil, p. 1]. Buenos Aires: 1877.   870

NETSCHER, P. M. List of Works on Brazil, [in Les Hollendais au Brezil, p. xi]. La Haye: 1853.   871

TRÜBNER, N. Bibliotheca Brazilica. London: 1878.   C 872

Chili.

BRUSEÑO. R. Estadistica Bibliográfica de la Letteratura Chilena. Santiago: 1862.   873

MARKHAM, C. R. Sources of information relative to Peru and Chili, [in No. 143, II, p. 573].   R 874

Colombia.

PINEDA, José Laureano ? Bibloteca de ex Coronel Pineda, or Collecion de las Publicaciones de la imprenta en el Virreinato de Santafé i en las Republicas de Colombia i Nueva Granada, de 1774 a 1850. Bogota, Granada: 1853.   875

Ecuador.

HERRERA, P. Esayo sobre la Historia de la Literatura Ecuatoriana. Quinto: 1860.   876

Guiana.

AVANGOUR, P. de. List of works relating to French Guiana, [in La France Rendu florissante par la Guyanne, p. 41]. Paris : 1852.
877

BIBLIOGRAPHY of French Guiana, [in Publications de la société d'études pour la colonisation de la Guyanne Français, No. 4, p. 576]. Paris: 1844.
878

LIST of works relating to Dutch Guiana, [in Catalogus de Surmanische koloniale Bibliotheck, p. 51], 'S Gravenhage: 1862.
879

Also in an earlier edition ; 1859.

NOUVION, V. de. Extraits des auteurs et voyageurs qui ont écrit sur la Guyane, suivis du Catalogue bibliographique de la Guyane. Paris: 1844.
880

SAINT-QUANTIN, A de. List of works on French Guiana, [in Guyanne Français, p. 105], by A. de Saint Quantin. Paris: 1858.
881

TERNAUX COMPANS, H. Bibliography of French Guiana, [in Notice Historique sur la Guyanne Français, p. 169]. Paris: 1843.
882

VENESS, W. T. List of Authorities on British Guiana, [in El Dorado ; or, British Guiana as a field for colonization]. London: 1867.
883

New Granada.

ACOSTA, J. Catalogue of books and mss. on New Grenada, [in Compendio historico de descubimiento y colonizacion de la Nueva Granada, p. 428]. Paris: 1848.
884

PINEDA. See No. 875.

VERGARA y Vergara, J. M. Historia de la literatura en Nueva Granada. Bogota: 1867.
885

Paraguay.

AZARA, F. de. List of works on Paraguay, [in Voyage dans l'Amérique Méridionale, p. 1]. Paris: 1809.
886

DALRYMPLE, A. Catalogue of Authors who have written on the Rio de la Plata, Paraguay, and Chaco. London: 1807.
887

DEMERSAY, L. A. Histoire ... du Paraguay accompagnie d'une Bibliographie. Paris: 1800.
888

MULHALL. See No. 847.

MURATORI, L. A. Bibliography of the Society of Jesuits in Paraguay, [in Il Cristianesinio felice nelle missioni, I, 5]. In Venizia : 1743.
889

Patagonia.

COAN, T. List of works on Patagonia, [in Adventures in Patagonia, p. 2]. New York : 1880.
890

QUESADA, V. G. Bibliography of Patagonia, [in La Patagonia, p. 657]. Buenos Aires: 1875.
891

Peru.

BIBLIOTHECA Peruviana. London: 1873.
C 891 (2)

CHAIX, P. List of works on Peru, [in Histoire de l'Amérique Méridionale, I, p. 339]. Genève: 1853.
892

CHAUMETTE DES FOSSÉS, A. Catalogue des livres. Paris: 1842.
893

MARKHAM, C. R. *See* No. 868.
— — Authorities on the Spanish Discovery and
Conquest of Peru, [in Life and Acts of Don A.
E. de Guzman, p. xix]. London: 1862.   894

SOLDAN, M. P. and M. F. Bibliography of
Peru, [in Geografia del Peru, I. 715], by M. P.
and M. F. P. Soldan. Paris: 1862.   895

Uruguay.

MULHALL. *See* No. 847.

Venezuela.

ROJAS, J. M. Biblioteca de Escritores Venezo-
lanos Contemporáneous. Caracas: 1875.   896

SPENCE, J. M. List of works relating to Venezuela, [in The Land of Bolivar, II, p. 271]. London: 1878.   897

WORKS relating to Venezuela, [in Catalogo de la
biblioteca de la universidad de Caracas]. Caracas: 1875.   L 898

Societies.

All college and state societies are given under
Political Divisions, and all scientific institutions
under the science.

Cincinnati.

See Nos. 472 and 478.

Colleges.

See No. 630.

Communistic.

NORDHOFF, C. Bibliography of Socialism and
Communism, [in The Communistic Societies of
the U. S., p. 421]. New York: 1875.   B 899

Hakluyt Society.

See No. 165.

Historical.

See also under each State.

GRIFFIN, A. P. C. Bibliography of the Histori-
cal Societies of The U. S., [in Mag. of Am.
Hist., XIV, pp. 106, 218, 418, 583, and 627].
New York: 1885.   B 900

WHITMORE, W. H. Bibliography of the various
Historical Societies throughout the United
States, [in Hist. Mag., XIV, 97]. Morrisania:
1868.   B 901

Jesuits.

See under Theology and Canada.

Masonic.

BARKER, J. G. Masonic Bibliography No. I,
[in Mass. Chronicle, Dec.]. Boston: 1877. 902

BARTHELMESS, R. Bibliographie der Freimau-
rerei in America. (Nachtrag zu der Bibliographie des Br. Kloss.) New York: 1856.   903

[GASSETT, H.] Catalogue of [Anti] Masonic
Books. Boston: 1852.   904

GOWANS, William. A Catalogue of Books on
Freemasonry, and kindred subjects. New
York: 1858.   C 905

Mormon.
See under Theology.

Oneida Community.
See Perfectionists *under* Theology.

Shaker.
See under Theology.

Smithsonian Institution.
See No. 273 (2).

Individual.

General Works.

BOON, Edward P. Catalogue of Biographical Pamphlets. New York: 1878.   C 906 *

GUERNSEY, R. S. Bibliography of the United States relating to Military Collective Biography. New York: 1874.   906 (2)

LEGGAT. Catalogue of Biographical Works, [no. 30]. New York: 1879.   C 907 *

MUNSELL, J. List of American Genealogy, Biography, and History. [Albany: 1888.]   C 908 |

ŒTTINGER, E. M. Bibliographie biographie universelle. Bruxelles: 1854.   B 909 *

ROORBACH, P. A. List of Biography. [in Bibliotheca Americana, p. 309]. New York: 1849.   B 910 *

RUSCHENBERGER, W. R. S. List of Biographical notices of fellows and doctors of the College of Physicians of Phila., [in an Acc. of the College of Phila., p. 292]. Philadelphia: 1887.   R 911

STONE, W. L. Biographical Writers and their Works, of the State of New York, [Proceedings of the N. Y. Hist. Soc. for 1845, p. 77]. New York: 1846.   R 912

WOODWARD, C. L. Catalogues of Genealogy, Nos. 11, 19, and 25. New York: 1878-83.   C 913 *

— — Bibliotheca Bloodandthunder. Catalogues of Trials, Nos. 4, 13, 17, and 24. New York: 1877-82.   C 914 *

— — 2700 Personals, Funeral Sermons, Eulogies, Biographical Sketches, Memorials, etc. New York: 1877.   C 915 *

WHITMORE, W. H. American Genealogist, being a Catalogue of Family Histories. Albany: 1875.   B 916 ‡
   Earlier editions 1862 and 1868.

Special Works.

ABBOTT, Lyman. Writings of, [in Literary World, XIV, p. 24].   917

ACOSTA, Joseph de. List of editions of, [in Naturale Histoire, I, p. xi]. By C. R. Markham. London: 1880.   918

ADAMS, John. *See* No. 497.

— John Quincy. *See* No. 501 (2).

ALEXANDER, Sir William. Bibliography of, [in Sir W. A. and American Colonization, p. 119]. By E. S. Slafter. Boston: 1873.   919

ALLEN, Rev. William. List of Writings, [in funeral "Discourse," p. 32]. By William B. Sprague. Albany: 1868.   920

i

ANDERSON, Alexander. A Brief Catalogue of Books illustrated with engravings by —. [Compiled by Evert A. Duyckinck.] New York: 1885.   921

ANDRE, John. Bibliography of, [in Mag. of Am. Hist., VIII, p. 61]. By J. C. Stockbridge. New York: 1882   922

ANGELL, Joseph K. Bibliographical Memoir of. By Sidney S. Rider, [in R. I. Hist. Tracts, No. 11]. Providence: 1880.   923

BAIRD, Spencer Fullerton. Publications of. By G. B. Goode. Bulletin Nat. Museum, No. 20. Washington: 1883.   924

BARLOW, Joel. List of his Published Writings, [in Life and Letters of J. B., p. 289]. By Charles Burr Todd. New York: 1886.   925

BOWDITCH, Dr. Nathaniel. List of his Scientific Writings, [in funeral " Discourse," p. 116]. By Alexander Young. Boston: 1838.   926

— — List of Reviews and smaller published Writings, [in " Eulogy," p. 94]. By John Pickering. Boston: 1838.   927

BRODHEAD, Jacob. List of his Published Writings, [in A Memorial of J. B., p. 52]. New York: 1855.   928

BUCHANAN, James. *See* No. 506 (2).

CABOT, John and Sebastian. Sources of Information relative to, [in No. 143, IV, p. 7]. By Charles Dean.   929

— — Bibliography of, [in Vie de J. and S. Cabot, p. 370]. By Henry Harrisse. Paris: 1883.
                                                           930

CASAS, Bartolome de las. A List of Printed Editions of the Works of. By Joseph Sabin. New York: 1870.   931

   Reprinted from Sabin's Dictionary. See also, on this subject, the Huth and Carter Brown Catalogues.

CASAS, Bartolome de las. Sources of Information Relative to, [in No. 143, II, p. 331]. By G. E. Ellis and J. Winsor.   932

— — Writings of, [in Coleccion de documentos Inéditos, p. 779]. por F. de V. D. J. Sancho Rayon y F. de Zabalburn. Madrid: 1879.
                                                           933

CHAMPLAIN, Samuel. Sources of Information Relative to. By E. F. Slafter, [in No. 145, IV, p. 130].   934

CHANNING, William Ellery. Reference List on, [in Library Journal, V, p. 112]. By W. E. Foster. New York: 1882.   935

CHAUNCY, Charles [1705–87]. A List of the Writings of Charles Chauncy. [By P. L. Ford. Brooklyn: 1884.   936

— — List of Writings of, [Funeral Sermon]. By John Clarke. Boston: 1787.   937

— — Same, [in Chauncy Memorial]. By W. C. Fowler. Boston: 1858.   938

CHILD, Lydia Maria. List of Works, [in " Letters of L. M. C.," p. 272]. Boston : 1883.
                                                           939

CLAY, Henry. Works by or Relating to, [in Norton's Lit. Gaz., III, p. 39]. New York: 1853.   939 (2)

COBBETT, William. Bibliographical List of William Cobbett's Publications. By Edward Smith, [in his " Biography of C."]. New York: 1883. 940
    Also in Waters' Life of Cobbett.

COLMAN, Benjamin. Catalogue of his Works, [in Life and Character of B. C.]. By Ebenezer Turrell. Boston: 1749. 941

COLUMBUS, Christopher. Dessertazione episto-lari bibliografiche sopra Colombo. By F. S. Cancellieri. Rome: 1809. 942

— — Excerpta Colombiana: bibliographie. Paris: 1886. 943

— — Bibliography of the First Letter of. By J. R. Major. London: 1872. 944

— — Bibliographical Appendix, [in Nicholas Syllacius, p. xxxv]. By James Lenox. New York: 1859. 945
    Also in Hist. Mag.

— — List of Editions of the Letters of Columbus, by J. Winsor, [in No. 145, II, p. 48]. 946

— — Lives and Notices of Columbus, by J. Winsor, [in No. 145, II, p. 62]. 947

— — Sources of Information Concerning Columbus, by J. Winsor, [in No. 145, II, p. 24]. 948

COLWELL, Stephen. List of the Writings of, [in Memoir]. By H. C. Carey. Philadelphia: 1872. 948 (2)

COOPER, James Fenimore. Bibliography of, [in Life of]. By T. R. Lounsbury. Boston: 1883. 948 (3)

CUMMINGS, Henry, D.D. Works of, [in funeral Sermon on]. By W. Allen. Boston: 1824. 948 (4)

CUNHA de Azeredo Continho, J. J. de. Writings of, [in Revista Trimensal de Hist. e Geog., Jan., 1840]. By J. da C. Barboza. Mexico: 1840. 949

CUSHMAN, Robert. Bibliography of the Sermon by, [in A Sermon preached at Plimmouth, in New England, p. xiii]. By Charles Deane. Boston: 1870. 950

DALL, William Healy. List of Papers by, 1866–1882. [Cambridge: 1883.] 951

DEANE, Dr. James. List of Writings, [in funeral "Address," p. 43]. By Henry I. Bowditch. Greenfield: 1858. 952

DE PEYSTER, J. Watts. Writings of, [on covers of " The Decisive Conflicts of the late Civil War," No. 3]. By J. Watts De Peyster. New York: 1867. 953

DRAPER, Prof. John William. Publications of, [in Nat. Acad. of Sciences Biographical Memoirs, II, 383]. By G. F. Barker. 1883. 954

DWIGHT, Timothy. Writings of, [in funeral Sermon, p. 34]. By Calvin Chapin. New Haven: 1817. 955

EDWARDS, Jonathan. List of his publications, [in Life and Character of J. E.]. Boston: 1765. 956
    Many other editions.

EMERSON, Ralph Waldo. Bibliography of, [in Literary World, XI, p. 183].　　926 (2)

— — [in Monthly Reference List, II, p. 17]. 957

— — [in " Memoriam "]. By A. Ireland. London: 1882.　　958

EVARTS, Jeremiah. Writings of, on the Indian Question, [in " Memoir," p. 431]. By E. C. Tracy. Boston: 1845.　　959

FILLMORE, Millard. *See* No. 506.

FIRMIN, Rev. Giles. List of publications, [in " Brief Memoir," p. 15]. By J. W. Dean. Boston: 1866.　　960

FORCROFT, Thomas. Bibliography of, [in 85th Annual Record of the Ancient and Honourable Artillery Co.] Boston: 1884.　　961

FRANKLIN, Benjamin. Catalogue of Works relating to, in the Boston Public Library. [By Lindsay Swift.] Boston: 1883.　　962

— — Bibliography of, [in Bigelow's Life of, III]. By J. Sabin. Philadelphia: 1879.　　963

— — Life and Writings, a Bibliographical Essay, by Henry Stevens. London: 1881.　　964

　Also in Historical Coll., I, and " 47th Cong. 1st Sess. Senate, Mis. Doc. No. 21."

GALLATIN, Albert. List of published and unpublished writings of, [in Writings of, III, 619]. By N. Adams. Philadelphia: 1879.　　965

GAY, Rev. Ebenezer. List of published Sermons, [in " Discourse," p. 35], by himself. Salem: 1822.　　966

GOMARA, Lopes de. List of editions of, [in No. 145, I, 169].　　967

GOODRICH, Samuel Griswold. List of works by, edited or spuriously accredited to, [in Recoll. of a Lifetime, II]. By S. G. Goodrich. New York: 1858.　　968

GRANT, Ulysses Simpson. Reference list on, [in Lit. News, VI, p. 243]. 1885.　　969

HAMILTON, Alexander. List of Books by, or Relating to, by P. L. Ford. New York: 1886.　　970

— — Influence of, [in Monthly Reference List, III].　　971

HAKLUYT, R. Writings and publications of, [in Divers Voyages, by R. H., p. xix]. Edited by J. W. Jones. London: 1850.　　972

HARRISON, William Henry. *See* No. 503.

— — Works relating to, [in Bib. of Ohio, p. 150]. By P. S. Thomson. Cincinnati: 1880. 972 (2)

HENNEPIN, Louis. List of the Editions of the Works of, by Joseph Sabin. New York: 1876.　　973

— Bibliography of, by J. G. Shea. New York: 1880.　　974

HERRERA, Antonio de. A List of the Editions of, by Joseph Sabin. New York: 1876.　　975

HOLLEY, Alexander L. Catalogue of his writings, [in Memorial of, p. 143]. New York: 188-.　　976

HOLMES, Oliver Wendell, [in Monthly Reference List, III, p. 17].　　977

HOOKER, Thomas. List of published works of, [in Walker's History of the first (Hartford) Church, p. 435]. By J. H. Trumbull. Hartford: 1884. 978

HORN, G. H. Entomological Writings of, by G. Dimmock. Cambridge: 1879. 979

HOUGH, Franklin Benjamin. Bibliography of the writings of, by J. H. Hickox. Washington: 1886. 980

HUDSON, Henry. *See* No. 148.

HULSIUS, Levinus. List of works written or edited by, [in Bib. Essay on Hulsius], by A. Asher. London: 1839. 981

HUTCHINSON, Gov. Thomas. Bibliographical Essay on. By Charles Deane. Boston: 1857. 982

    Also in Pro. of the Mass. Hist. Soc.

IRVING, Washington. Bibliography of, [in the Critic, III, p. 143]. By J. K. Pasko. March 31, 1883. 983

— — [in Monthly Ref. List, III, p. 12]. 984

JACKSON, Andrew. *See* No. 501.

— — List of publications relative to, [in Life of, I, p. xiii]. By James Parton. New York: 1860. 985

— — Authorities on, [in Life of Jackson, p. 387]. By W. G. Sumner. Boston: 1882. 986

JAMES, Henry, Sr. List of his published works, [in Literary Remains, p. 469]. Boston: 1885. 987

— — Jun. Writings of, [in Lit. World, XIV, p. 97]. 988

JEFFERSON, Thomas. *See* No. 498.

— — Bibliotheca Jeffersoniana, by H. B. Tomkins. New York: 1887. 989

KIRKLAND, John Thornton. List of Writings, [in "Discourse," p. 103]. By Alexander Young. Boston: 1840. 990

KNOX, John (1790–1858). List of writings of, [in Memorial of J. K., p. 119]. New York: 1858. 991

LATHROP, John, D.D. Writings of, [in funeral Sermon]. By F. Parkman. Boston: 1816. 992

LAWRENCE, J— ? The Entomological writings of. By G. Le Comte Dimmock. Cambridge: 1878. 993

LEA, Isaac. Published Writings of. By N. P. Scudder, [Bull. Nat. Mus., No. 23]. Washington: 1885. 994

LINCOLN, Abraham. A Memorial Lincoln Bibliography. Albany: 1870. 995

LIVINGSTON, William. List of Works, [in Sedgewick's Life of W. L., p. 448]. New York: 1833. 996

LONGFELLOW, Henry Wadsworth. The Longfellow Collector's Handbook. A Bibliography of first Editions. [By Beverly Chew]. New York: 1885. 997

— — Bibliography of, [in Literary World, XII, p. 87]. 998

— — [in Monthly Reference List, II]. 1882. 999

LOWELL, Rev. Charles. List of Publications of, [in Memoir, p. 37]. By L. M. Putnam. Cambridge: 1885.   1000

LOWELL, John, LL.D. Writings of, [in funeral Sermon]. By F. W. P. Greenwood. Boston: 1840.   1001

LUNT, William Parsons, D.D. Writings of, [in Memoir]. By N. L. Frothingham. Boston: 1002

McDOUGALL, Frances H. (Whipple). Bibliographical Memoir of. By Sidney S. Rider, [in R. I. Hist. Tracts, No. 11]. Providence: 1880.   1003

MADISON, James. *See* No. 499.

MARSH, George Perkins. Trial Bibliography of, 1801–1882. [in Lib. Journal, XI, 474]. By H. L. Koopman. New York: 1883.   1004

MATHER, Cotton. Bibliography of, [in Bio. Sketches of Harvard Univ.]. By J. L. Sibley. Boston: 1885.   1005

— — Writings of, [in Life of C. M.]. By S. Mather, Boston: 1729.   1006

MILLER, Rev. Samuel. (1809–1850.) Chronological List of publications, [in funeral " Discourse," p. 49]. By William B. Sprague. Albany: 1850.   1007

MONROE, James. *See* No. 500.

— — Bibliography of, [in Life, by D. C. Gilman, p. 253]. By J. F. Jameson. Boston: 1883.   1008

MORRIS, Gouverneur. Publications by. By Jared Sparks, [in Life and Writings of G. M., I, 519]. Boston: 1832.   1009

O'CALLAGHAN, Edmund Bailey. Publications of, [in Mag. of Am. Hist., p. 77]. By J. S. Shea. New York: 1880.   1010

OLMSTEAD, Denison. ·List of the principal Publications of, [in " Discourse," p. 31]. By Theodore D. Woolsey. New Haven: 1859.   1011

ONDERDONK, Henry, Jr. Writings of, [in Antiq. of the Parish Church, Jamaica, p. 163]. By H. Onderdonk, Jr. Jamaica: 1880.   1012

OSGOOD, Frances Sargent. Writings of, [in Literary World, XI, p. 141].   1013

— Rev. David. List of publications, [in funeral Sermon, p. 23]. By Abiel Holmes. Cambridge: 1822.   1014

OSSOLI, Margaret Fuller. Bibliography of, [in Life]. By T. W. Higginson. Boston: 1887.   1015

PACKARD, A. S. List of Publications of, [in Memoir of A. S. P., p. 89]. 1886.   1016

PAINE, Thomas. Writings of, [in Life of, p. 344]. By J. Cheetham. New York: 1809.   1017

PARKER, Joel. List of his published writings, [in a life of J. P., p. 26]. By George S. Hall. Cambridge: 1876.   1018

PAULDING, James K. Chronological List of Publications, [in Literary Life of, p. 393]. By W. I. Paulding. New York: 1867.　　　1019

POE, Edgar Allan. Bibliography of, [in Athenæum, July 29 and Aug. 5]. By J. M. Ingham and B. Forman. London: 1876.　　　1020

— — same, [in Life, Letters, and Opinions, II, p. 289]. By J. M. Ingham. London: 1880.　　　1021

— — [in Literary World, Dec. 16, XIII; p. 457]. Boston: 1883.　　　1022

POLK, James Knox. *See* No. 505.

PRENTISS, Thomas, D.D. Writings of, [in funeral Sermon]. By J. Bates. Dedham: 1814.　　　1023

PRINCE, Thomas. List of books by, [in Cat. of the American portion of the Library of T. P.]. By W. H. Whitmore. Boston: 1868.　　　1024

— — List of books by, [in Life of]. By S. G. Drake. Boston:　　　1025

PTOLEMY, Claudii. List of Editions of Ptolemy's Geography 1475–1730. [By W. Eames.] New York: 1886.　　　1026
　　　Also in No. 114, Vol. XVI.

— — List of Editions of Ptolemy's Geography, [in Historia Matheseos Universæ, p. 446]. By J. C. Heilbronner. Lipsiæ: 1742.　　　1027

— — A List of editions of Ptolemy's Geography, [in Catalogue of Labanoff de Rostoff, p. 4]. Paris: 1823.　　　1028

— — Litteraturæ geographie Ptolomeæ. By C. F. A. Nobbins. Lipsiæ: 1838.　　　1029

— — Bibliography of Ptolemy's Geography. By J. Windsor. Cambridge: 1884.　　　1030
　　　Also in Bull. of Harvard University.

RALEIGH, Sir Walter. The Bibliography of, By T. N. Brushfield. Plymouth: 1886.　　　1031

— — A Bibliography of Sir Walter Raleigh. [By Wilberforce Eames.] New York: 1886.　　　1032

— — Sources of information, relative to Sir Walter Raleigh. By W. W. Henry, [in No. 143, III, p. 121].　　　1033

— — References to works on, [in Notes and Queries, I, 138 and 252]. London: 1886.　　　1034

REED, John. List of Publications of, [in Sermon on his death, p. 15]. By R. M. Hodges. Cambridge: 1831.　　　1035

RODGERS, John. List of publications, [in "Memoirs," p. 342]. By S. Miller. New York: 1813.　　　1036

RUSH, Benjamin. Index of Subjects treated in his printed works, [in Eulogium on B. R., p. 92]. By D. Ramsay. Philadelphia: 1813.　　　1037

SCHAFF, Philip. Writings of, [in Literary World, XIV, p. 208].　　　1038

SCHÖNER, Johann. Bibliography of his Globe of 1523, [in J. S.]. By C. H. Coote. London: 1888.　　　1039

SEDGWICK, Catherine M. List of Works of, [in Life and Letters, p. 447]. By Mary E. Dewey. New York: 1871.　　　1040

SHEA, James Gilmary. Writings of, [in Trübner's Am. and Oriental Guide, No. 4, p. 69]. London: 1865.　　　1041

SHUFELDT, R. W. Bibliographical résumé of the writings of. By L. S. Foster. 188–. 1042

SIMMS, William Gillmore. Writings of, [in Literary World, XIII, p. 351]. 1043

SMITH, Rev. Henry. 1805–1879. List of writings of, [in "Memorial" of, p. 32]. Compiled by Joseph F. Tuttle. Cincinnati: 1879. 1044

— Capt. John. Bibliography of, [in Works of, p. cxxx]. By E. Arber. 1884. 1045

— John Lawrence. Writings of, [in sketch of his life]. By Benjamin Silliman. 1884. 1046

SNELL, Rev. Thomas. Writings of, [in "Memorial"]. Boston: 1862. 1047

SQUIER, Ephraim George. A List of Books, Pamphlets, and more important Contributions to Periodicals, etc. New York: 1876. 1048

STEVENS, Henry. A Catalogue of the Historical and Bibliographical Works of. London: 1885. 1049

— — List of his more important works, [in Booklore, III, p. 147]. By W. R. Credhead. London: 1886. 1050

STILLMAN, Rev. Samuel. List of publications, [in funeral Discourse, p. 32]. By Thomas Baldwin. Boston: [1807.] 1051

STOWE, Harriet Beecher. A Bibliography of Uncle Tom's Cabin, [in edition of]. By George Bullen. Boston: 1879. 1052

TAPPAN, David. Complete list of ↑ publications of, [in Sermons on import₂ . Subjects, by D. T., p. 24]. Boston: 1807. 1053

TAYLOR, Zachary. *See* No. 506.

THACHER, Thomas, D.D. Writings of, [in funeral sermon]. By S. Palmer. Boston: 1812. 1054

TYLER, John. *See* No. 503.

USSELINX, Willem. Bibliography of. By J. Franklin Jameson, [in Papers of Am. Hist. Ass. II, pp. 201–220]. New York: 1887. 1055

VAN BUREN, Martin. *See* No. 502.

VERRAZANO, Giovanni da. Bibliography of, [in Magazine of Am. Hist., Vol. VI, p. 68]. By B. F. De Costa. New York: 1881. 1056

VESPUCCIUS, Americus. Sources of information concerning, [in No. 153, II]. By J. Winsor. 1057

WARD, Rev. Nathaniel. Publications of, [in Memoir, p. 168]. By J. W. Dean. Albany: 1868. 1058

WASHINGTON, George. *See* No. 496(2).

— — Bibliographical List of books, [etc.] relating to the death of, by F. B. Hough. Albany: 1865. 1059
　　　Also in "Washingtoniana," II.

WEBSTER, Daniel. *See* No. 522.

— — [in Monthly Ref. Lists, II, 10]. 1060

— — Writings of and eulogies on, [in Norton's Literary Gaz , III, pp. 39 and 83]. New York: 1853. 1061

— — Bibliographia Websteriana, [in Bull. Mercantile Lib. of Phila., July]. By C. H. Hart. Philadelphia: 1883. 1062

— Noah. A Catalogue of Books by Noah Webster. [By P. L. and E. E. Ford]. Brooklyn, N. Y.: 1882. 1063

WHITTIER, John Greenleaf. Writings of, [in Literary World, VIII, p. 123].   1064
— — in Monthly Reference List, III, p. 3]. 1065

WHITE, William. List of his published and unpublished writings, [in Memoir, p. 305]. By Bird Wilson. Philadelphia: 1839.   1066

WIGGLESWORTH, Rev. Michael. List of Editions of Poems of, [in " Memoir," p. 141]. By J. W. Dean. Albany, N. Y.: 1871.   1067

WILLARD, Samuel. A Catalogue of his Works Published in his Life-time, [in "Compleat Body of Divinity, p. 915]. By Joseph Sewall and Thomas Prince. Boston: 1726.   1068

WILLIAMS, Catherine R. Bibliographical Memoir of. By Sidney S. Rider, [in R. I. Hist. Tracts]. Providence: 1880.   1069
— Roger. Writings of, [in Pub. of the Narragansett Club, I, p. 55]. By R. A. Guild. Providence: 1866.   1070

AUTHORS' INDEX.

www.ingramcontent.com/pod-product-compliance
Lightning Source LLC
Chambersburg PA
CBHW030613270326
41927CB00007B/1148